How Chicago's Scorin[g] [Cha]mp Slam-Dunked His [Way t]o Greatnes[s]

How does he do it? What's i[t that lets him] float through the air with the greatest of ease? Why does he do it? What is it that makes Michael feel playing hurt is better than not playing at all? Why does he pay any price to win? Does he have to win at all costs, or does he work hard and play hard because he hates to lose?

All the answers are here in this first-time, full-length book on Michael Jordan's public and private life—including a unique glossary of Jordan-ology!

MICHAEL JORDAN

MITCHELL KRUGEL

ST. MARTIN'S PRESS/NEW YORK

MICHAEL JORDAN

Copyright © 1988, 1989 by Mitchell Krugel.

Library of Congress Catalog Card Number: 87-63310

ISBN: 0-312-91697-3   Can. ISBN: 0-312-91698-1

Printed in the United States of America

First St. Martin's Press mass market edition/March 1988
First revised St. Martin's Press mass market edition/September 1989

10 9 8 7 6 5 4 3 2 1

For my parents, who gave me
everything I needed to make this book
possible.

And to Ilene, without whose love,
support, and lemonade I never would have
made it.

Contents

1.

Here Comes Mr. Jordan

AS HE MOVED TO HIS RIGHT AND DROVE the baseline, Michael Jordan prepared for a takeoff the Wright brothers and NASA never dreamed possible. In one giant step Jordan was about to elevate the game of basketball to new heights. The rim was now in full view but Kevin McHale, the powerful forward of the soon-to-be world-champion Boston Celtics, came into the picture and Jordan's path was blocked. So he merely spread his wings, glided under McHale to the back-door side of the basket, and, in one fell swoop, jammed the ball into oblivion. The look in McHale's eyes was undeniably reflective; he had just experienced suspended animation.

For the moment McHale may have thought he was seeing things, for what had just happened seemed incomprehensible. Jordan is that way: every day he does that head-shaking stuff, a simple leap in a single bound to steal the inbounds pass almost before it is airborne, which makes you look

1

at your brother and shake your head as if to say, "No way, man."

McHale soon learned seeing is believing when he watched Jordan do it to him again and again in the process of soaring to an NBA play-off record of 63 points on that April 20 afternoon in 1986. Only the flight patterns changed as Jordan provided an alternate perspective on the term *playing above the rim*. A drive and a left-handed dunk over Larry Bird, then a power cradle jam off the fast break. Finally he triple pumped, sliced between McHale and Robert Parish, and put in a reverse, over-the-shoulder scoop lay-up high off the glass to complete his repertoire. Who said man was not meant to fly?

Certainly the video footage of Jordan's frequent air raids ever since he catapulted into the national spotlight as a mere college freshman has been set to music in more than a few highlight films. Quintessentially speaking, Jordan is music in motion. This shy but eloquent individual who wags his tongue like a starving puppy dog every time he senses the rim is near has brought the game to a new level. As Jordan circled in and out of the rafters of basketball arenas across the country with the greatest of ease, he proved he is no fly-by-night phenomenon. If he didn't create a new era, he spawned a new genre. Once Jordan first entered into orbit, the gurus of the game watched him in midflight and collectively started shaking their heads; this was the dawning of the Age of Hang Time.

The in-your-face dictionary of dunk-ology defines *hang time* as "the amount of elapsed time a given object or person continuously soars at the peak of flight." Hang time was originally introduced into sports jargon as a noun denoting the flight of a football after it had been punted. Hang time was probably never meant for human modification until it was introduced into basketball vernacular, and now has been shortened to *hang* as is, "Hey, bro, did you see me hang on that fadeaway J?"

On the scale that measures hang time, Julius Erving and James Worthy are the standard; Dominique Wilkins and Spud Webb record Richter-like proportions. Jordan buries the needle. He has so much hang time it seems like he can fly. Even he has considered the idea, and when Pat O'Brien of CBS Television cornered him just before the start of the 1987 NBA all-star game to ask, "You really can fly?" this overly modest athlete replied, "Well, maybe a little bit." It's almost a case of which came first, the "Air" or the "Jordan."

Such a gifted athlete also happens to be graced or—as Michael himself would be the first to point out—blessed with good looks and an abundance of commercial appeal. His considerable fame is probably most visible in America's shoe stores and on its bedroom walls and playgrounds. There is a Jordan in living color, a poster-perfect image of his midair acrobatics covering the wallpaper. And check out the local school yard. There are the kids, decked out in black and red down to their toes, with a single sweatband set halfway up the left forearm, all trying to fly. To them, Jordan is an incredible hulk, the modern-day Captain Marvel.

Matt Doherty, Jordan's teammate at the University of North Carolina, once called him Superman when Jordan skied to jam over Ralph Sampson. After watching Jordan throw down his famous demoralizer dunk, on which the takeoff point is the foul line, Georgia Tech center Tim Harvey confirmed the moniker, saying, "I thought I was watching Superman." Even before his gold medal–winning performance in the 1984 Olympic Games, in which he was tabbed the greatest athlete in any sport, Jordan was the Greatest American Hero.

Though Jordan is on top of his profession, he seems oblivious to it all, or at least unaffected by stardom. Even in his quietest moments he maintains a friendly, unimposing demeanor. Sure it sounds corny, but Jordan is a down-home guy from Wilmington, North Carolina, where his mother, Delores, brought him up to have a kind word for everybody. He still is that way. Jordan's family ties are strong; in his first year as a pro he bought a satellite dish for his parents so they could keep track of him via cable television. Such had never been a problem before state-of-the-art technology; Delores and her husband James made it to every one of Michael's games through college, accompanying the team to such faraway places as Hawaii and Greece in the process. And the only one who has been able to shut down Jordan on the court in the last decade has been his mother: after the 1983 Pan-Am Games she confiscated his car keys to keep him from going to play in a pickup game while he was back home on vacation.

Even today what little time Michael takes for himself, he likes to spend on the golf course or hanging out at his suburban Chicago home with his brothers. Jordan may be one of the most giving professionals in professional sports. At times, his life seems like one long personal appearance, but it seems he has never turned down a request for an interview. In 1987 Jordan was named to the NBA's all-interview team, which is as much a tribute to his versatile talent as any of his other awards.

Quite simply, Jordan looks at life and realizes it's better to give than to receive. In his second professional game with the Chicago Bulls he scored 32 points, and afterward commented, "I'm just glad I could contribute to a victory." During his player-of-the-year caliber effort throughout the 1986–87 season Jordan soared like a Bird as he worked his late-in-the-game Magic. He scored the final 18 points, including a game-winning 18-foot jump shot with 2 seconds left against the New York Knicks in November 1986, and as he stayed to answer the last of an onslaught of questions, his last words were "As long as the team wins, everything is good."

Jordan is the consummate team player, a quality he also carries off the court. When his college roommate, Buzz Peterson, had to go home for a weekend to visit a sick aunt, Jordan cleaned the entire apartment. Peterson came back to find his bed made, his closet clean and his shoes and sweaters all in the right place. Apparently, Jordan does whatever it takes to win.

His affinity for winning is deep-rooted, just like all aspects of his personality. The big city has changed very little about him; he is and always will be from Wilmington. His first encounter with basketball was on the court behind his house, where his older brother Larry used to administer regular whippings. Jordan learned winning the hard way, and he originally chose the number 23 when he started playing at Laney High School in Wilmington because it was just over half of the number 45 Larry wore.

Perhaps, then, it was tradition rather than irony or coincidence that prompted Jordan's shot at the big time during his freshman season at North Carolina. In fact, as Jordan walked onto the court after a time-out had been called to set up the final shot in the 1982 national championship game, Tar Heel coach Dean Smith walked up to Jordan, slapped him on the butt, and said, "Knock it in, Michael." Seconds later, Jordan hit the game-winning jumper that seemed to be part of the master plan. During the next two years he would be named national college player of the year, and by the end of his junior season he was so head and shoulders above the competition, he left the college game to move on to a higher challenge. By the time he left college Jordan was playing head, shoulder, and elbows above the rim.

And if there was a master plan, a grand scheme of things for Jordan to develop his wealth of talent, the next marketplace after college figured to be the 1984 Olympics. Jordan proved to be the greatest player on the "single most talented collection of players ever," and the inevitable reactions to his prowess were as never before. After his team had just fallen victim to another of Jordan's air raids, Spain coach Antonio Diaz-Miguel called Jordan the most bewildering player he'd ever seen. And Bob Knight, the single greatest basketball coach in the world, who directed this U.S. Olympic team, put it succinctly: "He's a basketball player."

A hero's welcome and the accompanying ticker-tape shower naturally awaited Jordan after his Olympic performance, but it was nothing compared to the greeting he received upon arrival in the NBA. BULLS HOPE JORDAN'S A SAVIOR beamed the headline in one local newspaper, and on draft day 1984 there were more Chicago basketball fans in the grand ballroom of the Conrad Hilton Hotel than had been at a Bulls home game during either of the previous two seasons. It was an auspicious beginning, to say the least. With his initial reaction to becoming a member of a team that had lost 55 games over those past two seasons, Jordan immediately showed the Windy City his sense of humor: "Well, I don't think the Bulls will go undefeated next year." All of Chicago let out a collective laugh.

It didn't take long for Jordan to turn Chicago into his kind of town. With an ask-and-ye-shall-receive approach, Jordan has more or less built himself a Paytonesque following. His first appearance in the area was at a steamy high school gymnasium filled to the brim. He's had the locals hanging from the rafters ever since. Jordan's popularity is even visible with a trail of kids following him whenever he's in the public eye. He's had a Pied Piper effect on Chicago; but instead of music, Jordan has used hypnotizing dunks to lead the people on.

In a word, Jordan is fan-tastic. Other players have been similar local drawing cards, but no one has made an impact like Jordan when he takes his show on the road. He is as beloved in the Boston Garden as Bird, and he has a mecca in Milwaukee. Whenever he is on his way to the Forum, the Los Angeles freeways are even more backed up. People all over this land have had the pleasure of shaking their heads over Jordan's brilliance.

Former Milwaukee Bucks coach Don Nelson can only shake his head and laugh when he sees Jordan go around two and three defenders at a time to complete one of those arena-rocking jams. Sometimes that is the best way to handle things when Michael J. is playing against you; he has been a constant headache to more than one opposing coach. During the 1986–87 season Jordan skied to an average of 36.7 points per game, and there were times when teams used two defenders on him the entire game. The New York Knicks used three at one time—and lost. After Jordan scored 22 points against the Bucks in just his third game as a pro, Nelson said, "He's an absolute star, but it's unfair to compare him with Julius Erving because there'll never be another Doc." With all due respect, there will be a day when it will be unfair to compare Erving—or anyone—to Jordan. And to be sure, there isn't a player around the NBA who doesn't know what it's like to have Jordan dunk in his face.

The same select group also knows the difficulty of staying with Jordan drop-step for drop-step. To watch Jordan carve up a defense is a work of art. Says San Antonio Spurs guard Johnny Dawkins, a veteran foe of Jordan since his days at Duke, "Jordan goes all out. Not just physically, but he outthinks you. Back-door here. Lob to me here. Good defensive play there. Of all the players, he's the most impressive." Jordan relies on his hang time and his ability to maneuver the ball in midflight to score. It seems he loves to show the defender the rock, then use some sleight-of-hand to put it in the hole. In a split second he can change direction, square up, and hit a floating jumper. He also has considerable range with his shot; but then, given his choice, Jordan would just as soon cradle the rock between his wrist and forearm and jam.

And let's be honest, we'd all like to see him dunk too. Somehow, watching Jordan soar and score seems like a new and uplifting experience over and over again. He can dunk so many ways and does it so many times, he is the league's resident jam master.

The dunk is the single most glorious shot in all of basketball; no other moment in sport packs such explosion and energy into a split second. On the playground, the dude who can dunk is accorded instant respect. Jordan is the best of the best, having proved so by winning the 1987 NBA slam-dunk contest. Jordan has used said contest as a personal showcase for his vaunted dunk-orama, a virtual plethora of big stuffs, which like nothing else has created a nationwide obsession with his ability to fly without wings.

Clearly Jordan has been a hot commodity since he left college and became eligible to represent corporate America. This is one athlete who has the perfect commercial appeal. He could play basketball for free, and still make enough money to be a millionaire. Consider that the $800,000-plus the Bulls pay him in yearly salary is less than what he receives from McDonald's, Chevrolet, Coke, and Nike per annum. He is a company within himself, and all his hard work results in profits for Jordan Universal Marketing and Promotion, or JUMP, Inc. If his life is indeed one long personal appearance, he never seems to tire of it. "It's fun," he says. "The commercials and appearances—this is something you only get to do once in your life, so why not do it?" He is so sellable that when he came into the NBA, the Bulls created a whole new promotion and marketing department in order to cash in on Jordan's magnetism. The return on investment makes JUMP a Fortune 500 company. And let it be known that Jordan takes it upon himself to make sure no one—whether it be the corporate sponsor or the common fan—feels shortchanged.

As Tom Newell, onetime NBA scout, onetime college coach, and full-time guru once said, "There is one phenomenon in basketball, and his name is Michael Jordan." This is the story of that phenomenon.

2.

Home Is Where the Start Is

PERHAPS THE GREATEST LEARNING EXPER-
iences for young Michael Jordan were his daily
tête-à-têtes under the "rack" with his older brother Larry. On the court that James Jordan built for
his family, Michael suffered repeated beatings in
basketball's version of dueling known as one-on-
one. These were Michael's flying lessons, so to
speak, as he watched Larry sky to another victory.
Sometimes it was not a pretty sight: more often
than not Larry put it right in Michael's face. The
way Michael remembers, "It was like we were
playing opponents. We never thought of brother-
hood at all. Sometimes it would end in fighting."

Despite the outcome, there never was any love
lost. When Michael speaks of Larry now, it's with
all the regard that should be accorded an older
brother by his younger brother. "He's got the
dunks and some 360's and most all the same stuff I
got. And he's 5-foot-7. Larry is my inspiration."

Michael attributes everything he has and everything he is to his home, his hometown, and his family. Family is first with this James Gang, and Michael is just another one of the brothers, the second of five Jordan children. The parts of this clan make up the whole that is Michael. You see the outgoing nature, the good humor, the will to work hard in Michael; that's James Jordan. His compulsive competitiveness and will to win come from Delores. The ability to overcome all obstacles in a single bound no matter how overwhelming the situation? Well, that's something he picked on the backyard court along with a few scraped knees, a 360 slam, and hang time. No matter where Michael is in this land performing his brilliance, home is always where his heart is.

James Jordan has raised his family to live by and up to certain standards. He and Delores have always been upwardly mobile, and as Michael continues to climb the ladder of success he is merely following in the family tradition. Says James, "The way it is in our family, we try to make something happen, rather than waiting around for it to happen. We believe the surest way is to work toward making it the way you want."

James and Delores never waited for opportunity to come knocking. They each grew up down on the farm, where life as a sharecropper in Eastern North Carolina yielded little more than poverty. Talk about a long climb. In 1967, James took a job as a mechanic at General Electric's Wilmington plant, worked his way up through the ranks as a dispatcher and foreman, and eventually retired as a department supervisor. Delores started as a drive-in window teller at a branch of the United Carolina Bank, and she completed her climb by becoming the head of customer relations at the downtown office. Michael's burning desire to make the most of himself is as much a credit to his parents as anything else.

If James Jordan is driven—he built the court in back of the house from scratch by himself and he also built the house—then Michael is compelled. Here is a guy who was 5'9" when he entered high school, and probably better suited for baseball, having thrown more than a few Little League no-hitters. With his father and older brother barely pushing 5'7", basketball did not seem to be in Jordan's future. When he was a sophomore at Wilmington-Laney High School he was 5'11" and was cut from the varsity basketball team. As a junior he grew to 6'3", made the varsity, and made the people notice him. By the time he graduated he was 6'5" and standing tall. James can't quite understand why Michael blossomed like he did. "I think Michael just willed himself to grow."

There are those who have said Jordan was born to play basketball, but to put it more accurately, he grew up with the game. He also grew up an avid gamester, playing all sports and shooting an adept game of pool too. He learned to handle a deck of cards quite well and plays a great game of Monopoly. And from the time he learned to roll the dice, Jordan tried to do whatever he could to win.

For the most part, that's about the worst thing James and Delores ever had to worry about with Michael. Even when the principal called from Laney High to ask why Michael wasn't in biology class, James would ask, "Did you check the gym?" Jordan can hardly be blamed for having an affinity for dunking rather than dissecting, but after a second and third midday jam session, Jordan was eventually suspended from school. "I was a bad boy back then," he recalls.

If only he had just said no.

Ah, but Jordan had basketball in his blood; he was most definitely a junkie. And we can all be thankful he never kicked the habit, though being cut from the varsity as a sophomore while one of his best friends made the squad almost made Jordan think about withdrawal. He averaged 28 points a game as the junior varsity point guard, but even that didn't warrant being called up to the varsity at the end of the season for the state tournament. He did ride the team bus to regionals, but only because a team manager was sick, and since he didn't have a ticket he had to carry the uniform of the star player just to get in the gym. "At the time I vowed to myself to never let that happen again."

Now, of course, there isn't a player who can carry Jordan's jockstrap, as the saying goes. But he was hardly an overnight sensation. As Laney coach Clifton Herring put it, "He wasn't exactly the talk of Wilmington." But the coach knew enough to send Jordan to a basketball camp. And so it was that Herring started a letter-writing campaign to one of the game's greatest gurus, Howie Garfinkel, asking to let Jordan come to his Five-Star Camp, the one for the big-time college prospects, the blue-chippers, the can't-miss kids.

In this who's who of high school hoopsters Jordan was a no-name. But during the week he became the brightest of the stars by winning five individual trophies. He was invited back for a second all-star week and won four more trophies, which is still a Five-Star record. So if Jordan came to Five-Star as a suspect, he emerged as a big-time prospect, and more than a few colleges wanted Jordan to put his name on the dotted line of a letter-of-intent right there and then.

Jordan says that camp was "the turning point of my life." Not that he has ever needed a reason to work hard, but securing a college scholarship made Michael a man possessed. Every day during his senior season, Jordan would meet his coach at 6:00 A.M. and put in an hour of practice before school. Another two hours of practice after school, and then the day wasn't complete without a couple of quick games with Larry. By this time in his life, Michael had the upper hand, and the two would have gone at it all night if Delores hadn't called them in for supper.

Of course, Michael listened. He always listens to his mom and dad. When he was suspended from school, all James needed was to supply a few words of wisdom: "I told him, 'The way you are going, you will never get to college.'" Said Michael, "I knew he was right, and I knew I had to change." When Michael was pressing too hard at the beginning of his junior season in college and trying to live up to the fans' player-of-the-year expectations, he turned to his father to help him out of the prolonged slump. More simple words of advice: "You're trying to force things, son. Just play like Michael Jordan and things will fall into place."

It is important to Michael what his parents think. When he turned pro and bought his own home, he flew his parents into town to help decorate it. Quite simply, life isn't complete for Michael unless he can share it with his family. And it goes both

ways, for James and Delores and the rest of the clan
would go to the ends of the Earth for one another.

Delores and James have gone at least that far to
watch Michael play. Throughout his son's college
career, James went to every game, and Delores
missed just one. His younger sister, Rosalyn, graduated from Laney a year ahead of her class to join
Michael at North Carolina. At the start of every
college game, Jordan looked up to make sure his
family was in the stands. "If they're not there, a
part of me isn't there," he said once. Even today
before every game he looks into the television
cameras as if to say, "Hi, Mom."

Jordan is proud of his family, proud of his
heritage, proud of his hometown. Wilmington is a
coastal community of 56,000, hard by the Atlantic
Ocean. At the same time, Wilmington is deceptively large, yet deceptively small. It is large enough to
house considerable industry, yet small enough
where people know enough to know each other
and always have a friendly greeting for each other.
It is a world to itself. When outsiders ask what is
the biggest city closest to Wilmington, the locals
respond, "This is the biggest city." The people are
proud, and as one of its native sons, Michael never
hesitates to talk up his town. In 1985, Jordan was
about to go up against Atlanta's Dominique Wilkins, from nearby Washington, North Carolina, in
the finals of the NBA slam-dunk contest. When
asked about the competition, Jordan said, "He's
from Washington, I'm from Wilmington. As long as
one of the home boys wins, it doesn't matter."

Down home, Jordan can be himself. His favorite
source of relaxation is a trip back to Wilmington
where he can hang out on the corner with his

friends. Wilmington's leading commodity is its Southern hospitality, but its claim to fame is Michael Jordan. Says James: "When he comes home, people treat him like he's a god." Jordan lives in Chicago during the off-season because of the business opportunities available, but Wilmington is really his kind of town.

Jordan is a mama and papa's boy; the son of compulsive parents. A mere weekend at the Jordan home in Wilmington left a lasting impression on Buzz Peterson. "They made me feel at home." Adds James: "We've always looked on Michael's friends as our sons. We advise them as we do Michael." And what was it about the Jordan family that impressed Peterson the most? "They have so much love for each other."

There is never any love lost in this family.

3.

A Shot at the Big Time

THE MOMENT WAS SO PICTURE PERFECT IT has been captured on film and mass-produced all across North Carolina in the form of souvenir post cards. With 32 seconds left to play in the 1982 National Championship game, the Tar Heels trailed Georgetown, 62–61, when Jordan broke from the team huddle after a time-out and hustled on the court to meet his destiny.

On this star-struck evening in New Orleans, Jordan was not exactly the focus of attention. His All-American teammate James Worthy was having the game that night and already had scored 28 points, so the final shot figured to be his for the taking. Carolina coach Dean Smith realized Georgetown would be preoccupied with Worthy as well, so he instructed his players to take the first good shot. As point guard Jimmy Black faked a pass inside to freeze the Georgetown defense, it became apparent Jordan would have the first good shot, and such a move merely isolated him for the photographers. He went up with his body perfectly squared to the basket, as if to strike a pose, then swished a jump shot over Patrick Ewing and a bevy of flashbulbs.

The image is so vivid, people in Carolina have it committed to their photographic memories. The cover of the Chapel Hill–Carrboro telephone directory serves as a constant reminder. There is Jordan suspended high above Hoyas defenders Gene Smith, Larry Spriggs, and Ewing. The orange of the Superdome scoreboard reads N. CAROLINA on top 61, GEORGETOWN on the bottom 62. The clock ticked down to ":17" as Jordan prepared to pull the trigger.

You know, it's funny, but in the years after Jordan hit the shot no one really agrees as to how much time was left or how far out he shot from. Depending upon what you read, the moment came with anywhere from 15 to 18 seconds left. There are times when it was a 20-foot jumper, while it also has been written the shot was a 15-footer. Thank the Lord it's there in living color, for this is one case where a picture is indeed worth 1,000 words. In the years to come after the shot, though, it really didn't matter whether it was a 25-footer or a lay-up. It was the shot which rocked Jordan's world. "That kid has no idea what he's done," said Carolina assistant Eddie Folger right after the game. "He's part of history but he doesn't know it yet." Added James Jordan, "I knew our lives weren't going to be the same anymore."

That shot was just another day in the life of college for Michael Jordan. The day after, he was back in Chapel Hill playing in a pickup game. Even if Jordan had never done another thing for Carolina basketball, his picture would forever be hanging on the Tar Heel wall of fame. The shot had given Smith his first national championship, and from Asheville to Wilmington Jordan was given the keys to the cities.

There was, however, a time in his life when Jordan never wanted to play for the Tar Heels. In a state that is as fanatical about basketball as North Carolina, alliances and allegiances are inbred. All the talk about Hoosier hysteria is just mere folklore in this part of the country. Consider that all four major hoop-playing universities—Carolina, North Carolina State, Duke and North Carolina–Charlotte—have each been to the NCAA Final Four at least once since 1977. And growing up, Jordan was a State fan. "I hated North Carolina. David Thompson was the man," and it's almost as if Jordan patterned his game after the former Wolfpack skywalker who brought a national title home to the state in 1975.

Initially, Carolina wasn't too interested in Michael. Only during Jordan's junior season at Laney did Mike Brown, athletic director of the Wilmington school district and a Tar Heel alum, call Smith to tell him, "We might have a player down here." Jordan went to Smith's camp that summer, where he met Peterson and made a lasting impression on the coach himself.

While North Carolina noticed Jordan first, there was still a recruiting war to be fought. He made visits to both Chapel Hill, where Carolina is located, and Raleigh to see State. South Carolina entertained him at the governor's mansion. But then, during his senior year Jordan visited Chapel Hill with Project Uplift, a minority student program, and was hooked on the place people like to call Blue Heaven. "The coaches didn't even know I was here. I saw this place as a student, not as a recruit."

And let it be known that Michael Jordan came to North Carolina to be a student as well as a basketball player. He always, always went to class. When *Sports Illustrated* came to Chapel Hill to take pictures of him and teammate Sam Perkins for its college basketball preview issue in 1983, Jordan insisted they do a photo shoot in the classroom. Clearly, he knows the value of a good education. For sure, he knew his vocation would be basketball; but knowing he would spend so much time talking to television and newspaper reporters, Jordan made sure to take a speech communications class.

If there was ever any question about his dedication to his education, Jordan did go back and get his degree in geography even though he left Carolina after three years to turn pro. During that time he was almost as well respected in the classroom as he was on the basketball court. A solid B student, Jordan may have made the dean's list if he had had more time to devote to his studies. "He was definitely a competent student," said John Florin, Jordan's academic adviser and an associate professor in the university's geography department. "He had no trouble with the work, and he would have done better if he had had more time." Though life after basketball hasn't really been considered, Michael has said he would like to be a geography professor someday.

Jordan was just as much a student of the game, a class in which he was never anything less than an A student. Sure he had some trouble adjusting, and every college freshman reaches a point where he wonders if he can make it on this level. But any questions Jordan had were answered early; his initial test was a pickup game in Chapel Hill in which Michael was matched against the likes of Worthy, Al Wood, and Mitch Kupchak. He has total recall of the moment he first stepped to the head of the Carolina class.

"Al Wood was guarding me and it was tied, next basket wins. I had the ball, and I was nervous because people were watching and I wasn't sure I belonged out there. I drove the baseline and Al went with me. When I made my move to the hoop, [7-foot] Geoff Compton came over to help out. I went up and thought I was trapped. But I just kept going up and dunked over both of them. When I came down, I said to myself, 'Was that really me?'"

Even in college only seeing was believing with Jordan. The picture-perfect moments filled up more than a few walls by the time he finished. The accolades are aplenty. Jordan was named to enough All-America, Junior Olympic, Olympic, and AAU all-star teams to qualify for diplomatic immunity. Stories of his late-in-the game heroics are internationally renowned. When Carolina toured Greece the fall before Jordan's junior season, the Heels had to play a doubleheader one day. The second game went into overtime, and was threatening to go into double overtime. But with everyone else running on empty, Jordan kicked into high gear, stole an inbounds pass, and went the length of the court for a game-winning lay-up. His affinity for action when the game is on the line is legendary.

"It's the string that ties the package together," said Matt Doherty, one of Jordan's running mates in college. "He is the perfect player. When I grew up, I wanted to be 6-foot-7, and I wanted to be able to do anything on the court. I wanted to grow up to be Michael Jordan."

Jordan's performance during his freshman season—13.5 points, 4.4 rebounds per game, and rookie of the year in the ACC, not to mention his game-winning shot in the NCAA title tilt—was enough to make Smith and others nod their heads in approval. By his sophomore season, Jordan had people turning and shaking their heads. Now he was a player who belied ordinary statistics. New numbers games had to be created to evaluate his excellence. Suddenly, Jordan was being measured by how many points and rebounds and steals and blocked shots and game-saving shots he produced over two- and three-game periods. Smith had wanted more consistency on defense, so Jordan worked on it and won the team's defensive-player-of-the-game award 12 times during his sophomore season.

He finished that year averaging, per game, 20 points, 5.5 rebounds, 78 steals—a true player-of-the-year performance or so the *Sporting News* declared. Yet the most memorable moment of that season may have been Jordan's pickup of a loose ball and blind turnaround, desperation, 24-foot heave in the final 4 seconds to tie a game at Tulane that the Heels eventually won in triple overtime.

It was, however, during his freshman season when Jordan took his real shot at the big time. In reality that night in New Orleans may have been the first day of the rest of his basketball life. Not

only did it launch Jordan into the national spotlight, but it made him realize he didn't want to be a
one-hit-wonder. "I used to get tired of people
coming up to me and asking me about 'The Shot.' I
couldn't be Michael Jordan anymore. I was always
Michael Jordan who made the winning shot against
Georgetown. I didn't want to be remembered for
that shot. I wanted to be thought of as a complete
player."

By the end of his sophomore season, he was
thought of as *the* player. That summer he was the
leading scorer of the U.S. team that won the gold
medal in the Pan Am Games in Caracas, Venezuela,
and as Jordan went into his junior season, anyone
who knew anything about college basketball considered Jordan to be the player of the year.

Again, numbers do not do justice to Jordan.
Consider that Smith gave Jordan permission in his
junior season to free-lance on defense, and to leave
his man whenever he anticipated a steal or whenever he could create a double-team situation to
force a turnover. Only two other players at North
Carolina, Dudley Bradley and Charlie Scott, had
ever been allowed to free-lance. Billy Cunn-
ingham, James Worthy, Brad Daugherty, Phil Ford,
Mike O'Koren, and Sam Perkins are among the
Carolina all-Americans who were not. As with most
everything else he has accomplished, Jordan says
this is no big deal, but there are those who had no
trouble translating Jordan's brilliance into their
own words.

Said Smith before Jordan even began his junior
season; "He is so much better a player this year, it
isn't funny." When asked how or if Jordan could
be stopped, Clemson coach Bill Foster suggested,

"Grab his cape and hold on until help arrives." Perhaps the sign of the time Jordan was to have during his final collegiate season was his biography in the North Carolina media guide. The description merely began with "one of the greatest players in the game." Enough said.

Jordan quickly learned you can't believe everything you read. Four games into the 1983–84 season, he wasn't exactly making headlines. Though Carolina was undefeated, Jordan was averaging 14 points a game and grabbed a total of 11 rebounds. In two games he failed to pull down a single rebound. His game was lost in the translation. But the pictures said it all again. Jordan sat down with Smith in his office and watched film of himself playing both this year and the previous year. It was all there in black and white.

"I was trying too hard to live up to people's expectations, putting pressure on myself to be as good as they had said I was. I was reading too much about myself and paying too much attention to my statistics."

As soon as Jordan quit subscribing to other people's feelings, his numbers quickly came up. And how appropriate it was that Jordan kicked up his heels when Carolina opened the conference season against State. He scored 32 points in that game, and during the course of the final 22 games he averaged 21.7 points, 5.8 rebounds, while shooting 57 percent from the floor and 78 percent from the foul line.

And he saved his best performances for national television audiences. In the sixteenth game of the season, Carolina, undefeated and ranked number one in the country, was trailing LSU, 48–42, after a half in which Jordan was atypically quiet. Too quiet. In the quietest moment, Jordan exploded. Though he scored just 3 baskets in the first half, he started a second-half spree with a dunk off an alley-oop lob. He dashed off for another basket, then drove baseline, slammed, and was fouled. He converted the 3-point play, then capped off the run with a rousing dunk. In 1 minute and 37 seconds, Jordan put the Heels ahead for good and finished with 29 points.

In another nonconference game against Arkansas, he took the Razorbacks to the hole one-on-five. But nothing was as remarkable as what he pulled off to help the team clinch the ACC championship in a game at Maryland. Picture this: Guard Steve Hale dove for a loose ball going out of bounds, whipped an around-the-back pass to Jordan who cradle-jammed. He went on to score 13 points in the last 10 minutes and grabbed 12 rebounds in the process. During the final ten games of the conference season, Jordan averaged 24.1 points on 96-of-157 shooting from the field. And as Jordan was receiving player-of-the-year recognition by newspapers, magazines, and wire services coast-to-coast, Doherty was there to have the last words: "Michael was unreal. He just took over and put on a show for the nation." By the end of his junior season Jordan was not only player of the year; he was, in terms of playground lingo, All-World.

All the while, Chapel Hill and North Carolina remained his own little world. These are the pictures that Jordan will forever remember. In Chapel Hill there is a brick fence surrounding the library known as "The Wall" where Tar Heel basketball and football players hang around and joke with all the home boys. The memories Jordan has of passing the time with Lawrence Taylor, Kelvin Bryant, Wood, Worthy, Perkins, and Peterson could fill a photo album.

And then there are the stories they tell. Peterson and Jordan have a tale all their own. These are two guys who met at Smith's summer camp, formed a friendship at Five-Star, and became the closest of roommates in a state where some people still shake their heads at the idea of a black and white player living together. Yet the chronicles of Peterson, who is from Asheville, and Jordan running together are legendary. They turned double dates into two-on-two Monopoly games. Peterson turned Jordan on to golf; while Jordan, in turn, showed his friend the ins and outs of pool. Their battles persisted in everything from backgammon to cards. They are at home with each other's families, and each describes the other as "like a brother to me."

Clearly, there is a part of his life in Chapel Hill Jordan likes to relive whenever possible. He had a clause put in his professional contract that requires the Bulls to play one exhibition game in town every year. At the same time, Jordan gets a chance to go back to The Wall, and be at home. "It's very comfortable there," he says. To him, that's the big time.

4.

Olympic Hero

BY THE SUMMER OF 1984 IT WAS AIR APPAR-
ent Jordan was going to lead a life saturated with
great moments. He was already a national hero,
and even the most uninformed basketball fan could
provide a shot-by-shot description of his brief, yet
eventful career. And so it was on a steamy August
evening in Los Angeles that Jordan went about
providing the next thrilling episode. This was an
Olympic moment. He exploded past half-court of
the Los Angeles Forum as if he were invading the
enemy, which happened to be a shell-shocked
team from Spain. Jordan was airborne at the foul
line, at which point he cradled the ball and gave
Spain's Fernando Martin an up-close-personal view
of his rock-the-baby, over-the-shoulder, reverse
slam. This was a momentous occasion, to be sure;
Michael had arrived as an international phenomenon. And after he helped reestablish U.S. domi-
nance of Olympic basketball in a big way, stories of
his greatness spread worldwide. By the end of

these Games, word of Jordan was spanning the globe; from Australia to Zimbabwe he was being called the greatest athlete in any sport. One of the Olympic gurus suggested placing Jordan and Daley Thompson of Great Britain, the decathlon champion, in the middle of the Coliseum, giving them a ball and a jug of Gatorade, and letting them create their own game. For Michael this truly was his golden moment.

Jordan is still very proud of his 1984 gold medal, which is displayed very prominently in his living room. But never had a medal and an Olympic hero been so anticipated. Due in large part to media hype, Jordan's lot as the greatest amateur player in the game was cast almost a year before his Olympic moments. His play in the 1983 Pan-Am Games and the following collegiate season had people hanging their tongues in excitement. Never had a victory tour been so awaited since another Michael J. set his music in motion. As always, Jordan was up to the task; he figured if the glove was being thrown down, he'd be there to answer the challenge.

For a time during his junior season at North Carolina even he couldn't pick up a magazine or a newspaper without seeing himself identified as "future-Olympic-hero Michael Jordan." As the boys on the bus jumped on the Jordan bandwagon, they put it in print that Michael's Olympic stardom was a given. The rave reviews started after Jordan led the U.S. on its steamroller mission to the gold medal in the 1983 Pan-American Games in Caracas, Venezuela, and from that point on it was difficult to hold the press.

Michael, of course, never has been one to believe everything he reads, so the Olympics was merely one more forum for him to leave a lasting impression on the nation. And it was right there, just outside of Hollywood, that Michael looked at his abilities and realized, "That's entertainment."

"Even though people knew me before the Olympics, things have been different since then," he says. "Since then, things have taken off. The Olympics gave me more exposure than anything I've ever done."

Some of the 72 players who ventured to Bloomington, Indiana, in April of 1984 for the Olympic team tryouts could have done without their overexposure to Jordan. This adventure, which Indiana coach Bob Knight conducted as if it were part marathon, part boot camp, became affectionately known as a trial by fire, and it was Jordan who was burning bright in the end. Jordan had already made a career of rising to the occasion, but in front of a collage of college coaches and a melange of NBA scouts it was just another opportunity for Jordan to stand up and be touted.

For purposes of organization, Knight and his committee of assistant coaches categorized the multitude of talent into positions after each day's series of workouts. There were guards, forwards, and centers; and then there was Jordan. His classification became *Miscellaneous*, for on any given day he'd move from point guard to big forward and back again. Only in this arena did it become evident how gifted Jordan was. While some of the game's other greatest players had their moments, Michael was consistently spectacular. Whenever Knight wanted to test a player's offense, he made him go one-on-one against Jordan. His status high above the rest was so established that he went through the trial virtually unmentioned. Apparently, even then there were no words to describe Michael.

Despite Knight's insistent claims that no single player had made the squad before the trials, Jordan was a lock. There were times when Knight could have pulled four people out of the stands, put them in uniform and sent them out to play with Jordan, and the U.S. still would have posted a 36.7 average margin of victory. Leon Wood, the U.S. team point guard who set up Michael for his alley-oop slams, explained just how good Jordan was in the Olympics: "I talked with other athletes who have been watching our games, and a lot of them said Michael is the best athlete in any sport, from any country. I told them, 'You ain't seen nothing yet.'"

Even seeing wasn't believing, for there were those who played against Jordan that to this day will swear they only saw a blur and the ball go by them en route to the basket. He blazed a trail of shaking heads through the Olympic Village all the way to the land of the Rising Sun and the Land Down Under. But for the three weeks of the Games, this land was his land, and there were times when giving Jordan the rock and clearing the court to let him strut his stuffs would have been a better show than what transpired during the L.A. Massacre. His wizardry near Westwood made Olympic basketball a demonstration sport if there ever was one: synchronized overkill, as one astute bystander observed.

Jordan's presence made basketball the hottest ticket in town, and he proceeded to put on an unforgettable performance for all those involved. In the 91–47 opening-game rout of China, Jordan struck for 14 points on a series of baseline beauties and demonstrative dunks. There were times when judges could have been brought in from the diving competition in order to evaluate his degree of difficulty.

The next night Canada was the representative from "Victims International," and Jordan went to work as soon as the curtain went up. He ignited a 22–6 U.S. spurt during the first eight minutes with eight riveting points. The rattle of the rim was lost in the noise of the crowd, but Jordan left them roaring with a 20-point extravaganza. The entire U.S. team was something to cheer about in this 89–68 win, but in the end even Canadian guard Eli Pasquale realized, "We just couldn't stay with Jordan."

If exclamation is the sincerest form of flattery, then a fitting tribute to Jordan's Olympian onslaught were the words of praise he drew. After Michael contributed 16 points to a 104–68 victory over Uruguay to give the U.S. team a 3–0 record in the Games, 'Guays coach Ramon Etchamendi said, "Maybe we have chance playing seven against five." Clearly Jordan made Etchamendi feel thoroughly undermanned.

The crowning achievement was Michael's 24-point outing in a 101–68 decimation of Spain, a performance almost beyond description. Jordan hit 12-of-14 shots from the field and scored 18 points in the first half, the last 2 on a fall-away, 30-foot, desperation jumper at the halftime buzzer. He slashed through the Spanish defense, making the opponents seem more like matadors than basketball players.

Afterward Spain coach Antonio Diaz-Miguel had trouble finding the proper words of praise. "He's like a robot. He's not a man." But even that was mistranslated. "Not *robot*," the interpreter clarified, "he meant *rubber*." Same difference.

Diaz continued to elaborate on his feelings: "He is the most bewildering player I've ever seen. I asked my good friend Bob [Knight] if he want my whole team in trade for Michael Jordan. He no want." Added Spain's Martin, "Jump, jump, jump. Very quick. Very fast. Very, very good. Jump, jump, jump."

The feeling was mutual throughout the competition. Said West Germany's Christian Welp, "We just didn't want them to beat us by 50 or 60 points." Jordan, who was selected to be captain of the team, finished the Olympics as the leading scorer with a 17.1 average, and in Knight's regimented, restricted system he was only unleashed for brief spasms. Still, Knight, the man who truly deserves the title *mentor*, understated "He's a basketball player." That's with the emphasis on *player*. But even the overimposing Knight found a place in his heart for Jordan after sharing the Olympic moments. Knight walked into the locker room before the start of the gold-medal game against Spain, wondering if his team was up to this task. He approached the blackboard to write down starting assignments. Taped to the board was a note from Jordan reading, *Coach, after everything we've been through, there is no way we're going to lose this game.* Knight still has the note.

When all was said and won, U.S. assistant coach George Raveling added, "In two or three years there will be a major controversy in the NBA. It will concern how Michael Jordan was allowed to be drafted only third instead of first or second."

The Olympics provided the first of many golden moments for Michael Jordan.

5.

Third Pick Is a Charm

THE CHICAGO BULLS WERE MIRED IN A seemingly endless no-win situation in the spring of 1984 when fate smiled on them in a peculiar way. Or was it that fate stuck its tongue out at this problematic franchise?

It became evident that the Bulls were on the verge of being one of the worst teams in the NBA that year. But a paltry 27–55 record may have been the best season the team has ever experienced. The reward for such futility was the third selection in the NBA's college draft, which for the Bulls was like winning the Lotto. The third pick in the draft in 1984—the one after Akeem Abdul Olajuwon and Sam Bowie, if you can believe it—was a real jewel.

Michael Jordan was still flipping a coin in indecision as he made his way to Dean Smith's office the morning of April 15, 1984, the last day he could declare hardship and become eligible for the draft. But it was a relatively easy decision for Jordan to

forgo his final year of college basketball to move
into a higher tax bracket.

"I feel like it's time for me to move on," Jordan
explained. "Money plays a big part in each of our
lives. Who knows? I may not be around next year. I
think it's better to start now. For timing's sake and
the future, it was time for me to go." Added Smith:
"There's no gamble this way."

So when Michael sat down with the coach to
ultimately make the decision, he put the coin in his
back pocket. Heads he won; tails he didn't lose.

In previous years it seemed the Bulls had re-
sorted to something as rudimentary as flipping
coins to make the draft picks. Here they were, a
team comprised completely of number-one draft
picks and backup centers, struggling to win more
than 25 games. And this time around, for some
strange reason, there was still some question about
picking Michael when draft day came. As Bulls
general manager Rod Thorn would explain later,
"He's a very good offensive player, but not an
overpowering offensive player. Michael was too
good a player to pass up."

Can you imagine passing up Michael Jordan?
Jack Ramsey, who was the coach of the Portland
Trailblazers, the team which drafted Bowie sec-
ond, still can't believe they passed up Jordan.
Suffice to say, it's a good thing the Bulls had no
choice.

This was a no-lose situation to be sure, and
Chicagoans were more than ready for a coming-out
party. Chicago's famous delicatessens already had
an item on the menu in anticipation of Jordan
becoming a Bull: the hero sandwich. More fans
packed the grand ballroom of the Conrad Hilton

Hotel that afternoon than had been at any single Bulls game the two seasons before. Even as Olajuwon and Bowie realized their fortunes, the windy city began echoing "Jordan, Jordan" loud enough for Bulls management to hear two floors above. Shortly after noon (CST) on June 20, the fans got what they wanted. And while everyone was rejoicing in the moment, Thorn said, "Jordan isn't going to turn this franchise around. I wouldn't ask him to."

It didn't take long for Michael to turn heads in Chicago and make them start shaking. He was greeted with the standard reverence and revelry, and Jordan left them laughing. After learning he had been the Bulls' choice, Michael, who had never been on a losing team and had lost but two games in his final season at North Carolina, said, "Well, I don't think the Bulls will go undefeated next season." But he was equally as excited as the fans. "I'm anxious to meet the team and start fitting in with them." The handwriting was on the wall, and Mike Thibault, a Bulls assistant coach at the time, saw it. "He's one of those players who comes along once in a decade."

The official greeting party was something that takes place once in a lifetime. Jordan's local debut in a Bulls uniform was a coronation more than anything else. The victory tour took off at Washington High School's steamy gymnasium October 9 in East Chicago, Indiana, where the public reaction confirmed Michael J. was in town. By the end of the evening, a throng of screaming teenage girls seemed intent upon tearing away his uniform. "Michael Jackson, eat your heart out," said teammate Orlando Woolridge. "Those girls were screaming, weren't they? You got to love it." Jordan eventually had to wave a white glove and retreat to save his skin, let alone his clothes.

But what was more significant about this night was that this exhibition game against the Milwaukee Bucks drew a capacity crowd of 5,000, even though it was the night of the first game of the World Series and even though the Bucks had traded away East Chicago native Junior Bridgeman the week before. Jordan was simply dazzling in the process of scoring 22 points. The Bucks' Sidney Moncrief, the NBA's defensive player of the year the season before, was assigned to Jordan on this night, but even he couldn't keep up with Michael's first step—or any of his subsequent ones, for that matter. "No problem," said Jordan of his first-period confrontation with Moncrief. "As long as we win, everything is good."

It was the third time all was great and all was good for the Bulls during this exhibition season. The third game was a charm every bit as much as the first two, considering the Bulls were 3–0. It seemed Jordan had turned around the franchise. "Michael does a lot for this team, especially bringing a winning attitude," Woolridge continued. "That's something we tried to find around here before, and we couldn't make it. But Michael has been a catalyst, the type of player who makes everyone around him look good." All this, and Jordan had been a pro for just three games.

But even in his second game, Jordan played like an old pro. In a 107–100 victory over Kansas City, Michael hit 10-of-11 shots from the field and 12-of-13 from the foul line on his way to a preseason high of 32 points. This was a sign of the times for the Bulls. Through six games of the exhibition season the Bulls were 5–1 and Jordan had averaged 22.3 points in just 29 minutes of play per game. As Chicago finished the preseason with a 5–2 mark, Jordan led the team in scoring with a 22.7 clip on 59.2 percent shooting from the field. Once more, he pulled down 5.3 rebounds per game—third-best on the team—and had a total of 14 assists, 9 steals, and 6 blocked shots. He did everything asked of him and more, including playing four positions—point guard, big guard, small forward, and big forward—and even guarded players as tall as 6-foot-10.

All of which had Thorn singing a completely different tune. "The only player I would have taken ahead of Michael Jordan is Akeem Olajuwon," said the Bulls GM as the exhibition season came to a close. "It will be nice to have a player like him in a Bulls uniform. I don't want to put too much pressure on him, but there are certain guys who seem to bring out the best in their teammates. I think Michael Jordan has the potential to be like that. He is a terrific offensive player—a great, great player."

Greatness can be measured in terms of innovation. The truly great ones are usually accompanied by the phrase *the first time* throughout their careers, as in "This is the first time a player has ever taken off from the foul line for the 360-degree dunk" or "This is the first time a player has ever scored 40 points in 10 consecutive games." Jordan already had many firsts by the time he became a Chicago Bull, but with the addition of their franchise player, this would be the first time the Bulls would ever build an entire advertising campaign around one player.

As Jordan had previously pointed out, timing is everything, and the time was right for him to become Chicago's newest hero. The Cubs, baseball's perennial heartbreakers, had just choked away a two-game lead and lost out to the San Diego Padres in the National League Championship Series. Clearly, the time was right for Jordan to make the scene.

But even before Jordan arrived in Chicago, the Bulls were selling themselves as "A Whole New Breed." The campaign featured Jordan at his most appealing. In addition to television commercials, full-page advertisements ran in the local newspapers promising "Here Comes Mr. Jordan." It was a play on the 1941 classic film starring Robert Montgomery, and the ad called it "his first starring role since the Olympics." Half of the space was devoted to rave reviews by everyone from Bobby Knight to Gene Siskel, who gave Michael a four-star rating. The ad reminded, "Playing locally for 41 nights only," which is how many home games the Bulls had scheduled for the season.

The only one reluctant to place Jordan on such a pedestal was Jordan, because he always wants to share the limelight. In the NBA, modesty can often be the mother of attention, but Jordan made sure to point out that the Bulls' new winning ways— indeed, the whole new breed—was something he contributed to, rather than inspired.

"I don't want to overshadow anyone. I knew everybody's eyes would be on me when I came into the league. I'm trying to play my natural game, and I think I'm establishing myself, gaining the respect of the players. Maybe my personality can inspire the other guys. It's a good way to get everybody laughing and feeling good about the game.

"This doesn't feel like a losing team. Everyone knows I hate to lose, and I spread that feeling among the team by the way I play. My number-one goal this season is to help make this basketball team into a winner. And I want to have fun."

Bulls center Dave Corzine added the other point of view: "Michael gave everyone a lift. He didn't loaf, and he was so good, he couldn't create jealousies. It's obvious to see the change he can make in the team."

And it was a time for a change. The entire city, not to mention the franchise, needed a shot in the arm, and Jordan provided the right medicine. Within seven games of the exhibition season Jordan had Bulls fans on a natural high. Even the men in the three-piece suits were exchanging high-fives after seeing Jordan strut his stuffs. "I don't think a person came away feeling he didn't get his money's worth watching Michael," said Bulls coach Kevin Loughery. "That's what makes him special. People come out to watch because of the hype, and they find themselves wanting to come back again."

Jordan's power plays turned on the fans, the coaches, and his teammates. Already he was demonstrating an energy that would eventually light up the NBA. "He has an amazing flow of adrenaline," Woolridge said. "When he runs and leaps in practice, we all want to try to run and leap with him even if we're tired. Now the excitement level within the team is incredible. I'm so enthusiastic about what he can do for us that my wife gets tired of hearing me talk about him.''

But he already was the talk of the town. It was as if all of Chicago had collectively thrown a coin into a fountain and wished for the Bulls to get Jordan. And everyone flipped over him.

6.

National Phenomenon

SPECTATORS STAMPEDED THROUGH THE aisles of Madison Square Garden, trying to move closer to the visitor's basket in order to get a close-up view. Michael Jordan was throwing down some demonstrative dunks, and the local reaction seemed to say, "Yes, it is alive." He started with a whirlwind 360, then came a swooping, shaking one-hander, followed by a two-hand power jam. The exhibition culminated with a show-it-left, show-it-right whirling dervish. And Michael was merely warming up. With 26 seconds left in this NBA game in October of 1984, Jordan picked the pocket of Knicks guard Darrell Walker, headed off toward the basket, cradled the ball in one hand, and shook it twice before completing a slam that left New Yorkers with their tongues hanging.

Across the great divide, less than a week later, Jordan made a similar great defensive play against San Diego's Norm Nixon to force an air ball. Bulls center Caldwell Jones retrieved the shot and hit

Michael with a pass at midcourt. As he zeroed in on the basket, the Clippers' Derek Smith wrapped up Jordan in a bear hug, which was about the only way to bring him down. But as Jordan was falling and sprawling he kept his arms free and floated the ball softly off the glass and into the basket. One enamored Clipper fan rose to his feet to give Jordan his due and began shouting, "U-S-A, U-S-A." It was as if Jordan returned to the Olympic City to stage a personal closing ceremony.

Coast to coast, Jordan was becoming the toast of every town he played in. Once again he was creating a phenomenon that could be described in no certain terms. The numbers game that is figuring attendance in the stadiums of the NBA provided tangible evidence, but there was no real accounting for what Michael was doing to this nation.

Or what the nation was doing to him.

There was the usual stuff any celebrity has to deal with: the hours of repetitive interviews, answering the same questions from the press after every game; the police escort to and from every personal appearance, which still isn't enough to keep the girls from screaming and crying and trying to tear off your clothes; and the donning of disguises and dark glasses to have a little privacy in public. In such a situation, one also is required to maintain a low profile so society won't misinterpret isolated incidents and get the wrong idea. And, of course, there is the persistent demand to make TV commercials and to pose for posters and advertisements.

And then there was the sublime which megastars often face: signing autographs on everything from popcorn boxes to bare skin; going away for the weekend and coming back to find 49 messages on the telephone answering machine. And being a role model means avoiding the bad reaction and the confrontations—even fighting—because you don't want to set a bad example.

And there was also the ridiculous. As he became a national hero, a day in Michael's life meant such extremes as appearing at the local auto show or speaking at the local athlete-of-the-year banquet in addition to practice and the press. Going out to see a movie only resulted in having to sign autographs by usher's flashlight. And only superstars the caliber of Michael Jackson, Elvis, and perhaps Joan Collins have to deal with an enamored fan throwing himself in front of a moving limousine just to get an autograph.

Michael was only a rookie, but already he was the single most unifying force among America's young people. Magic had the bulk of his following in Los Angeles and perhaps Michigan, while Bird was a hero to those kids in Boston and perhaps the small towns of Indiana. But there isn't a basketball-playing youngster around the country who hasn't wanted to lace up his or her Air Jordans, push a wrist band halfway up the forearm, and stick out their tongues while attempting to fly. Check it out: all the Michael Jordan clones—black or white or yellow or red—on the playgrounds, in the back-yards, or down at the community centers. Less than one month into his professional career, and he was as loved in the Felt Forum as he was in the Fabulous Forum; as cheered in the Garden—Boston or Madison—as he was in the Meadow-lands.

Proof positive rests in the libraries of this country. Yes, you can look it up, but don't expect to find anything. Paging through copies of *Sports Illustrated*, the *Sporting News*, or even *Jet* yields nothing. Someone has ripped out or ripped off every written word and picture of Michael, which are now part of personal scrapbooks or affixed to bedroom walls.

A mark of true national acclaim, however, is how prevalent a player's number becomes. Bird and Jabbar made 33 a top seller, while Doctor J's 6 graces the back of more than a few jerseys. The number 44 has always been considered to be worn by a superstar, while Magic has made 32 quite visible. But as soon as Jordan began trashing every rim in America, any boy or girl who made his or her grade school, junior high, or high school team wanted to wear number 23.

"He was like a good cancer," Woolridge said. "It has spread from person to person, coast to coast. Even I want to be able to dunk like he can." The reaction was the same in Orlando, Florida, as it was in Oakland. "The kid is something special," echoed more than one member of the media.

And Michael took it all in stride. "A lot of people want to know what I'm like, what kind of person I am, what I'm thinking. Yeah, it gets tiring, the same stuff over and over. I know I have to do it; I want to do it. That's when I push myself."

Yet it's the fans' reaction that seems to light up Jordan and it's for them that he lights it up. "It gives me such a warm feeling. Basketball, all my fans, they have given a lot to me. This is my way of giving something back to the community. I won't have any problem keeping the crowd pleased. Playing basketball is fun."

Michael was becoming a source of endless enjoyment and entertainment for so many. Jack Nicholson, a fine entertainer in his own right, is perhaps the best known NBA fan in the world. His courtside seat at Los Angeles Lakers games is legendary. Whenever the Lakers are at home and on television, you see Jack almost as much as Magic and Kareem. His love of basketball and the Lakers is so renowned that in its promotion campaign to prompt interest—"NBA Action is Fan-tastic"—the television commercials feature a shot of Nicholson walking to his seat right after Michael dunking and just before Bird hitting a shot from behind the backboard. But when the Bulls came to Los Angeles to play the Clippers on their West Coast trip in 1984, Nicholson did the unthinkable by forgoing a Lakers–Sacramento Kings game on that night to catch Jordan's act. The Clippers also drew more than the Lakers—14,366 to 12,766—on that night, the only time such an occurrence happens every year. It was also the Clippers' second-largest crowd of the year. One can only imagine what drew the largest crowd into the L.A. Sports Arena; perhaps a free concert after a game by Lionel Richie or the Temptations. But whether it is Jordan jamming the rock or some rock star jamming, that's entertainment.

From the beginning of his rookie season Michael exhibited the youthful enthusiasm and charm that virtually won over the crowd everywhere he played. The Bulls' first trip to Detroit to play the Pistons was the epitome of what he does to the hometown boys. He jumped over Pistons forward Terry Tyler not once, but twice, in the process of consecutive slams. The second brought the house to its feet, and when he jammed off an alley-oop pass from Wes Mathews, it brought the house down. Jordan finished the exhibition with another slam, which prompted a standing ovation.

But nothing short of a coronation could match what happened when Jordan made his first stop in Dallas. For the 129 days prior to Michael's arrival, Dallas sportscaster Dale Hansen of WFAA-TV counted down the time to Jordan's local lift-off. He teased the fans with nightly highlights of Jordan's air raids on his sports cast, touching off the biggest hype in Dallas since Bobby Ewing came back to life. Or Patrick Ewing. But this was no dream. "We turned a great basketball game into an event," said Dallas general manager Norm Sonju after seeing the crowd herd into Reunion Arena. "This is absolutely amazing," Hansen added. "Nobody in Dallas shows up on time; not for Cowboys games, not for anything. And this place was filled half an hour before the game." Hansen further related that local scalpers usually get up to $100 a ticket when the likes of Bird, Magic, and the Doctor come to town. But for this particular game the going scalper's rate was $225 per seat.

These days, though, the pinnacle of any athlete's national popularity very well could be appearing as a guest on "Late Night with David Letterman." Jordan was accorded such fame and handled Dave's best lines very admirably. When the host asked Michael about his Air Jordan shoes, and why they were banned from the NBA (more about that later), Jordan merely answered, "Well, they don't have any white in them." Dave replied, "Neither does the NBA." Laugh, riot, Michael found a new way to turn on the nation.

Television land wanted to get as much of a piece of Jordan as possible. The respective networks of the NBA, CBS, and Superstation WTBS out of Atlanta had scheduled 65 regular season telecasts between them during the 1984–85 season, but only once were the Bulls featured. In comparison, WGN, the Chicago Superstation, had plans to televise 15 Bulls games and early in the season the network was drawing 30,000 more households than it did for its telecasts at the same time in 1983. The numbers were up so much that CBS tried to switch its traditional Philadelphia–Detroit Thanksgiving Day game to Philadelphia–Chicago, but the NBA denied such a request. Commissioner David Stern did, however, ask WTBS to try and squeeze another Chicago game into its schedule, and he prompted a commitment from CBS to televise the Bulls if and when they were in the play-offs.

Jordan was more than the main man; he was the main attraction. For his efforts during the first four weeks as a pro, he was really a shoo-in for the NBA's rookie-of-the-month award, and suddenly the Bulls became the fourth-best draw on the road in the league, averaging more than 13,000 a game. The onslaught was so great, a member of the Bulls' public relations department had to be with Jordan every step of the way.

But this was a case where numbers, for a change, belied Jordan. On the Bulls' West Coast trip,

Jordan sold out the house in Los Angeles, Portland, and Golden State, a rarity for the latter. In New York 15,239 showed up to see his warm-up during the exhibition season, and 19,252 came back with their mouths watering for Jordan's second visit. "Are we the home team?" Walker wondered.

And the beat went on. A sellout crowd of 15,542 came to see this mecca in Milwaukee, while the Pontiac Silverdome was filled to brim with 19,252 when Chicago visited Detroit. When the show stopped in Indianapolis, 16,920 packed Market Square Arena, the fifth-largest crowd in Pacers history, which dates all the way back to the beginnings of the American Basketball Association. "With that tongue hanging out, he seems like such a happy player," uttered one Pacer fan even though Jordan had hit the jumper to give the Bulls a 118–116 victory.

The Bulls were one of the league's worst road shows in 1983–84. But with Jordan to top the marquee, Chicago sold out 8 of its first 13 road appearances. Back home, the Bulls had averaged 6,365 a game in the years B.M. (Before Michael), but now they were drawing 12,763 a game to the Chicago Stadium.

Everywhere, however, it was always the same scene. Michael would take the court and throw down some dunks to bring the crowd to its feet. Then he'd hit a couple of fall-away jumpers or block a few shots to get them roaring for more. Finally, he would defy the laws of gravity in the process of making shots no man had ever taken before. When all was said and won, Michael had won a place in every fan's heart. With Erving on his way out, Jordan was just what the doctor ordered to bring the fervor back to the NBA. Sometimes, seemingly for good measure, he'd hit the fans with one of his improvised on-the-spot, showtime jams.

Ah yes, that's entertainment.

7.

Rookie of the Year

EVERYWHERE HE WENT, MICHAEL STOLE
the show, or so it seemed. Only the scenes of the
crimes changed as Jordan concentrated on protect-
ing his innocence. But he was quickly becoming
one of the NBA's most wanted; the man with his
picture plastered on the walls of arenas across the
country. He was above the laws of the land, in
addition to his competition. It was as if Michael's
alarming performances had all the effect of a
dragnet on the game. And he had the "rap" sheet
to accompany such stature, a virtual hit list of
quick jobs which left people shaking their heads
even after the smoke had cleared.

These are just the facts, ma'am:

After scoring 45 points in his ninth game as a
pro, Michael made off with a page in the Bulls
record book—the one that listed the top scoring
performances in a single game. His fingerprints
were found on another page after Jordan exploded
for 22 points in the final quarter of a win over

Milwaukee. When he canned a 20-foot desperation jumper at the final buzzer to deliver a 95–93 win over the New York Knicks, there were accusations that he stole the spotlight. The Knicks were thinking more in terms of grand larceny: as in, Jordan stole the game.

The beat went on. Jordan scored 45 points in a win over Cleveland, then came back the next night with 42 points on 16-of-25 shooting from the field before 17,865 witnesses at Madison Square Garden. Suddenly it was 45 points one night against Atlanta, 41 back home against Boston, and 49 in a victory over Detroit, and Michael was clearly establishing himself as one of the untouchables. The evidence continued mounting up: Twice he was named the NBA's rookie of the month, and twice he was chosen the league's player of the week. Seven times he broke the 40-point barrier; 30 points was no barrier to him.

Was it legal? Was it fair? Sure, even as rookies, Magic and Bird had rolled up big numbers. But not until either reached the top of their games did they create the statistic known as a "triple-double." A triple-double occurs when one player reaches double figures in the three major statistical categories—points, rebounds, and assists—in any single game. Magic and Bird had reached such a plateau sporadically in their first few years. But Jordan did it twice in his first five months as a pro. Already, opposing players and coaches were complaining that the refs were letting him travel, an honor that isn't normally accorded a rookie.

But this was no ordinary rookie. Jordan was a surprise beyond his years. A rookie like Michael hadn't come along in years. In the past, the feeling among the fans was that it takes a thief for the Bulls to steal a victory. But Jordan came through with the goods just about every time he was called on to do the job. He was a second-story man in the truest sense, because that's the level he played on when compared with the rest of the competition. Only a rookie and he was the "man" in the NBA. And as the song says, "You don't want no trouble with the man." Or something like that.

He was arguably the best rookie in the league, and by the end of the season such a debate would be an open-and-stuff case. And with his first basket as a professional, Jordan didn't leave much room for doubt. After taking a pass at the top of the lane, he used a spin move and a crossover dribble to create space with which to take off. While he was still going up, the others were coming down and Jordan calmly laid the ball in the hoop. The roar of the crowd ruled in his favor. And they hadn't seen anything yet.

Six games into the regular season and Jordan had nothing left to prove. It was on October 30 at the Chicago Stadium against Milwaukee that Jordan would be magnificent until proven guilty. More than 9,000 fans were on hand to serve as judge and jury, and there would be no appeal to this verdict. Michael scored 22 of his game-high 37 points in the fourth quarter, including 20 of the Bulls' final 26 in the 116–110 triumph. His double-pumping glides to the basket not only produced three-point plays but induced Paul Pressey and Alton Lister of the Bucks into fouling out in the waning moments. Jordan's pair of free throws down the stretch iced the victory, and bettered by one point the team record set by Bob Love for most points in a quarter

in 1972. It also proved Jordan was capable of
taking matters into his own hands when the game
was on the line.

"He was sensational," said Milwaukee coach
Don Nelson. "Down the stretch, we couldn't do
anything with him. We tried double-teaming him,
and he just jumped right over it."

Jordan added his own testimony: "We just
needed some enthusiasm in the fourth quarter to
get everything going."

The testimonials were all his to be had, and it
would be most difficult not to describe his continued exploits with glittering generalities. But perhaps teammate Sidney Green put it best when he
said, "He's the truth, the whole truth, and nothing
but the truth." As Jordan used a series of swoops
and scoops to score 45 points in a 120–117 victory
over San Antonio, he demonstrated he was capable
of doing the little things as well as the big-time
stuffs. With the Bulls ahead 113–110, there was a
jump-ball situation. Just before referee Jake
O'Donnell tossed up the ball, Jordan moved to the
spot where he thought the tip would go. Moments
later he was racing down court to an uncontested
lay-up. In fact, the only pursuit he would have on
this night was on a breakaway jam fest in which
Woolridge trailed him all the way, mimicking
every move.

And that picture deserved a few more words.
"Michael plays with so much pizzazz and electrici-
ty," Woolridge said. "He plays with so much
enthusiasm, it keeps everyone else pumped up."
Added Bulls center Dave Corzine, "Michael
couldn't do any more than he's done for us so far.
The way he pulls people up in the clutch. Every-

one on the team gets caught up in his emotion. It's unbelievable. He can do it all. When he can get those people to cheer for me, he's a magician." As always, Bulls GM Rod Thorn had the last words: "Nobody knew Michael would play this well as quickly as he has. He's been a tremendous player from day one."

Wonders never ceased. Just when his teammates, coaches, management, and the fans thought Michael had done it all, he did it again. Just when the media was about to write him off as being tired, Jordan would come right back with his best shot. With time running out in a December 8 game against the Knicks, Michael canned a 20-foot buzzer-beater to pull out a 95–93 victory. A few nights later, he soared for 32 points, including 14 in the second quarter, in leading the Bulls to a 110–85 victory over Boston, the worst defeat the defending world-champion Celtics had suffered in two seasons.

Michael was a man for all seasons; not one to get lost in the spirit of things. After taking a couple days off during the Christmas holidays to visit the folks in Wilmington, he came back to score 45 points and added 11 assists, 7 rebounds, and 3 steals in a 112–108 win over Cleveland. He scored 29 of those points in the second half, and seemed to give the crowd a Christmas present in the form of 6 slam dunks. The crowning achievement was a cradle jam on which he shook the ball twice like a pair of dice just before stuffing it through. He closed out the third quarter with two consecutive slams. Yes, Michael was on a roll.

And with the stadium rocking and rolling, you could tell Michael really loves the home cooking.

"I was able to relax and see my family, which I really wanted to do," he said of his trip home. "My mom cooked me turkey and yams, but she wouldn't let me touch a basketball. I wanted to shoot around a little, but she said no. After tonight, maybe she knew something. You know what they say: Mother knows best."

With Jordan, the Bulls were no longer a bunch of mama's boys. In the first two-and-a-half months of Michael's first season, Chicago had beaten the Lakers in Los Angeles and the Pistons in Detroit. The Bulls handled the Bucks at home and they had beaten the Celtics. The season had already been called one long roller-coaster ride, but the team was on the right track. With Jordan soaring and scoring, there would be enough highs to overcome the lows. With Michael on their side, the Bulls were clearly a better team, and if the jury was still out, Michael continued to pile up the evidence.

Exhibit A was a three-game swoop in which Jordan proved he was not tiring out even as winter moved into its dog days. In a January 14 victory over Denver, Michael compiled 35 points, 15 assists, and 14 rebounds, the first triple-double in Bulls history. In the process, he proved he could beat opponents with his head every bit as much as his heart. During the first meeting between the two teams, Denver's T.R. Dunn held Michael to 17 points. But Michael had a plan this time around. While the Nuggets concentrated on him, he became a setup man. "I knew everyone would be looking for me, but I didn't want to get all the points. I knew my teammates could score. My tactic worked out. When they started cracking down on them, I sneaked in to score." Perhaps then it was only appropriate that Jordan score his one thousandth point as a professional in this game.

He continued to make his point with 38 points and 12 rebounds in a 110–107 loss at Indianapolis. Jordan exhibited his ability to turn on his game when the game was on the line. He scored 15 in the last quarter and sparked the team's final flurry with 7 points in 4 minutes, which brought the Bulls to within 2, 85–83. As one local sportswriter observed, "It's Michael Jordan against the Indiana Pacers, and Jordan's winning."

The closing arguments came in the form of a 32-point, 12-rebound outing in a win over Portland and a 45-points, 10-rebounds, 8-assists effort on a sprained ankle in a triumph over Atlanta, all of which sealed Jordan as the choice for "Rookie of the Month" for the second time that season. "I've been really pushing myself," stated Michael as he took the stand on his own behalf. "People say I will get burned out, but I'm not the type of person to pace myself. I have to play my hardest every time on the court. A lot of people say I might not last the season. Well, just wait and see."

Case closed.

The verdict came from a jury of his peers. Michael, who had repeatedly said he would be happy just to play in one all-star game during his career, was named as a starter for the 1985 extravaganza in Indianapolis. He would be the first rookie to start since Isiah Thomas in 1982, and even though Michael was but a rookie, it was evident he had to be included among the legends of the game. Joining Jordan and Thomas as starters for the Eastern Conference were Moses Malone, Larry Bird, and Julius Erving. "I'll be playing with four

hall-of-famers who have already proven themselves," Michael said in awe. Make that five, for in
just half-a-season Jordan proved himself worthy of
such company.

And Michael was more than impressed to be so
judged. "It's outrageous. Remember when I said
one of my goals was to play in one all-star game?
I'm going to be so nervous. I probably won't
remember how to play. I may not score a point."

And always one to want to give the people their
money's worth on an occasion such as this, he
added that, "I've got some things I haven't done in
front of people yet. But I've got to get out and
practice them." The all-star game and accompanying NBA slam-dunk contest the day before the
game provided a forum for Jordan to strut his
stuffs. He did so in the process of taking second to
Atlanta's Dominique "The Human Highlight
Film" Wilkins in the slam-dunk competition, but
the game itself was not exactly one that provided
much video footage of Michael. He scored but 7
points on 2-of-9 shooting from the floor and 3-of-4
from the foul line and had 2 assists and 1 turnover
in 22 minutes of play.

There was almost an eerie feeling. Sweaty palms,
parched throats, turning stomachs, knees weaken-
ing. Jordan wasn't himself. "I've never had that
feeling before," Michael said. "I didn't feel like
myself. I've never been as nervous."

Oh well, chalk it up as another first-time-ever in
Michael's career, and not the "freeze out" some
say the more veteran members of the East team
were supposed to be conspiring to out of jealousy
of Michael. There were stories that Michael was
perceived by the other NBA superstars as being

cocky or arrogant for such trivialities as wearing his gold chains during the final round of the slam-dunk competition. But as Michael pointed out about the game, "I was very tentative." Chalk it up to experience; as has always been the case with Jordan, there is a first time for everything.

He is foremost when it comes to firsts. At midseason, he was leading the team in scoring, assists, steals, and blocked shots. He was second to power-forward Steve Johnson in rebounding. He had brought fun and the fans back to the stadium, and he had made a meandering franchise a play-off contender. What more could he do?

He could lead the Bulls to the promised land, the land of Moses, Magic, and the Celtics. Only a rookie of this prototype could be counted on to make the players around him better. But that's what Jordan, who always aims to please, aimed to do. With the Bulls having problems rebounding, he issued a challenge to the team's big men that he was going to try to beat them out for the team lead. And one day after practice, he sat in front of his locker figuring ways to motivate his teammates. As if scoring 45 points on a sprained ankle wasn't inspiring enough.

"By me challenging them, it will force them to work harder, and it will be good for competition." The reaction was completely positive. Jordan's presence was opening things up for everyone. Woolridge was becoming a force at small forward, while Quintin Daily was "getting rich" off the outside shots opponents' double- and triple-teaming of Jordan created. And as Jordan scored 49 in a victory over the Pistons, everyone got in on the act. Daily had 21, while forward Sidney Green came off the bench to score 16 points and pull down 15 rebounds. Dave Corzine played inspired defense in closing off the middle.

The Bulls were streaking toward their first play-off appearance in seven years, their second in the past nine, and Jordan fueled their fire. He put together streaks of mathematical proportions in the stretch run. Speaking of streaking, Jordan went one week in March with 92 points, 27 rebounds, and 25 assists in three games. His second triple-double —21 points, 10 rebounds, and 10 assists—against New York was followed by a 39-points, 9-rebounds, and 8-assists performance against Washington. A few nights later he scored 32 points and added 8 assists against Detroit. In four straight games he scored 30 or more points, and his 35 in a victory over Cleveland gave him 2,043 for the season, a Bulls record. The Bulls beat Boston 107–104 in Boston behind 33 points from Michael, and the most important 25 of the year came in a 100–91 win over Washington, which clinched a play-off berth for the Bulls.

Afterward David Greenwood called the team into the shower, where the players crowded around Jordan and doused him with beer, apparently as a toast to the success he brought to the franchise. "The beer was my idea," Greenwood said. "He carried this team at times when the guys couldn't carry themselves. This was a toast to Michael. He ain't a rookie no more."

Michael had come of age. Eventually the Bulls would fall victim to their own youthful enthusiasm in the play-offs and lose to Milwaukee, three games to one, in the best-of-five, opening-round series. But Michael left them clapping as he scored 35 points, including a jumper with 17 seconds left to give the Bulls their only victory of the play-offs, by a 109–107 count. Jordan finished as the league's third-leading scorer with a 28.2 average and fourth in steals with 2.39 per game, and he walked away with the NBA rookie-of-the-year award by more than 20 votes over Houston's Olajuwon. And that was proof positive that Jordan was one of those players who didn't come along every year. From now on, everywhere Michael went, he would be holding court.

8.

The Selling of a Superstar

AT THIS POINT IN HIS CAREER, THE BASKET-
ball court wasn't the only place to catch a glimpse
of Jordan's sky-walking. On the outskirts of town
stood that billboard, as if it were part of the
horizon, beaming that larger-than-life image of
Michael clad in his "Air" apparel floating toward a
basket. Or flip on the television, and there would
be Michael soaring toward a playground hoop, all
the while asking us in a deep voice, "Who said
man was not meant to fly?" Change the channel
and you might see Michael swishing a 20-foot jump
shot right through the sunroof of his Chevy Blazer.
A further flip of the switch might find him with a
Coke and a smile catching the wave with Max
Headroom. He certainly is the real thing.

In addition to everything else, Jordan is God-
gifted with tremendous commercial appeal. He is
articulate, bright, and good-looking, especially
when he is wearing one of his favorite Italian suits
from Bigsby & Kruthers. He is not camera-shy, and

he knows how to please the public. He has the right touch of down-home personality and warmth, and he's simplistic enough that he doesn't make people feel threatened, intimidated, or uneasy. And that smile. Well, that's worth a million dollars in itself.

Even before he ever set foot in the National Basketball Association it was obvious Jordan was mass-marketable. During his final year at North Carolina, an entourage of photographers from *Life* magazine spent an entire afternoon setting up the crest of a grassy hill on campus with a basketball hoop to do a photo shoot of Michael for the magazine's pre-Olympic issue. And his Olympic heroics only served to make Jordan an even hotter commodity.

Which brings us to the overwhelming question: What price fame? It would take some highly creative cost analysis to put a number on Jordan's head, for the way he has reeled in the dollars with his array of promotions and endorsements, not to mention his ability to play the game, almost makes no sense. (Or is that cents?) He doesn't have an agent; he has a team of attorneys, advisers, investment counselors, estate planners, public relations people, and agents. ProServ, Inc., handles Michael, and he has proved to be so marketable that all his enterprises had to be incorporated under the name Jordan Universal Marketing and Promotion: JUMP, Inc., for short. ProServ has made Jordan the most sellable sports star ever, and, at the same time, made sure he is financially secure for the rest of his life.

But Michael seems to be in it for more than the money. Consider that he has given us "Air Jordan," which has completely saturated America's athletic society. Now there is even "Air Jordan Express," a complete athletic outfitter, where we can purchase all of our Air Jordan attire. America's basketball players have one unifying characteristic it seems. They all want to look like and be like Michael Jordan.

To the Bulls, Michael is the franchise. As soon as Jordan was drafted, Jonathon Kovler, the Bulls' current managing partner, completely restructured his organization. Suddenly the Bulls had a director of promotions and the staff was enlarged in the marketing department. The organization began selling Michael Jordan long before he ever put on a Bulls uniform, and the return on investment belies the most creative accounting. Suffice to say, Jordan has brought new meaning to macro economics. When you look at his list of enterprising activities it reads like a financial statement.

When Jordan speaks of his association with ProServ, he refers to them as "my attorneys." He doesn't like the concept of an agent, the man who negotiates your contract and takes 20 percent off the top, and he doesn't like the idea of having "people." When someone asks him if he can make a speaking engagement, Michael doesn't want to have to say, "I don't know, you'll have to talk to my people."

But after Jordan declared himself eligible for the NBA draft, he knew he would need someone to represent him financially and legally. He could have picked any sports management agency he wanted. But Michael made sure to be penny wise rather than foolish with his future. He made sure not to throw his money away. He consulted with

Dean Smith and before the draft he presented six or seven potential representatives with a hypothetical scenario of what team he might go to and what the salary might be. Then he asked how they would handle it.

David Falk, ProServ's senior vice president in its Washington, D.C., office, appealed to Jordan's intelligence in money matters. He presented Michael with ideas for investments and planning for his career after basketball. Jordan was sold. As a result of ProServ's management, Jordan earned three times more in endorsements, royalties, and personal appearance fees during fiscal year 1986 than the $600,000 salary he was paid for playing basketball. Today there is a poster in Falk's office inscribed "Thanks for everything." The undersigned is Michael Jordan.

But Jordan may never be able to thank ProServ enough. The company is exactly what Michael was looking for in his effort to avoid all the shysters who pretend to be agents. ProServ, which annually takes in more than $100 million, was created in 1969 by Donald Dell, a former tennis star, to represent tennis players. The first clients were Dell's Davis Cup teammates, Arthur Ashe and Stan Smith.

The principle of the company is to handle every financial responsibility from paying the client's taxes to making his house and car payments. The total management concept is the new genre in representing sports stars. The client is given an allowance and doesn't have to worry about paying the bills. All the while he is learning financial management.

ProServ has two hundred individual clients, including Jimmy Connors and Dave Winfield, in addition to more than fifty corporate clients. The agency has offices in Paris, London, Bologna, Sydney, Tokyo, Dallas, San Francisco, and New York, along with Washington, D.C. The firm works so closely with its clientele that the relationships extend beyond business. Falk, for example, has Adrian Dantley of the Detroit Pistons as the godfather of his daughter.

"It's kind of a fatherlike situation," Jordan says. "I'm friendly with the people at ProServ outside of business, as well. If I want something, they do have to give it to me. I do have to talk to them, though, about all the clothes I bought in Europe, but they're always taking care of business."

In Jordan, ProServ realized a rare business opportunity. His All-American status in college, combined with his Olympic moments and a charismatic personality that is as electrifying as one of his air raids on the rim, made Jordan a no-risk, high-yield investment. His hardworking habits and relentless effort would be conducive to the long hours it takes to make commercials and prepare other promotional paraphernalia. The demand for Michael's supply of talent was already there. "Michael Jordan," said Donald Dell as Michael was about to enter the professional market, "has a charisma that transcends sport. He belongs in a category with Arnold Palmer and Arthur Ashe." But he was about to move into a category—and a tax bracket— all by himself.

When Michael signed a contract with the Nike shoe company, it was one small step for him into the world of promotion, but it was a giant leap for his popularity. When he first put on those Air

Jordan high tops suddenly everyone wanted to follow in his footsteps. It was Air Jordan that enabled Michael Jordan to get off the ground.

The whole concept was conceived on a humid 1984 afternoon in Washington several weeks before Jordan was to report for his first training camp with the Bulls. Falk was meeting with an old friend, Rob Strasser, a representative of Nike. Times had been tough for Nike lately; the running boom was slowing down and an unsuccessful adventure into the apparel market left the company in need of a new endeavor.

The basketball shoe market was definitely saturated; Converse, Adidas, Pony, New Balance, and Etonic each had the big names of the game promoting their products. Every player had a shoe contract with one company or another. But nobody was dominating the market. Since basketball shoes double as leisure shoes that kids like to wear around the school yard, any new venture had to be fashion conscious.

Falk and Strasser agreed that the market could be penetrated by signing a few major stars and backing them with major advertising dollars and television time. In the meantime, Falk was thinking about a shoe contract for Jordan. He knew Jordan would be able to command a primo offer from just about any company, but here with Nike was the possibility of the greatest shoe contract ever. Strasser went on to explain about Nike's new air-insole—an innovation in the construction of high tops to add extra padding to the sole of the shoe, which not coincidentally would facilitate flying—and about its interest in the apparel market.

"Air Jordan," Falk resounded immediately. Consider that moment not only the launching of Jordan's involvement with Nike but the takeoff point for his entire promotional career.

Strasser went back to Nike headquarters in Beaverton, Oregon, and sold the executives on Air Jordan. Jordan came to Beaverton with his parents, where he viewed a videotape of himself running and dunking and soaring and scoring and blocking shots to the tune of "Jump" by the Pointer Sisters. That was the first Michael ever heard of Air Jordan and about a clothing line reflecting his charisma.

Jordan was sold, too. The final deal from Nike afforded him $2.5 million over five years in addition to royalties on each item sold and a long-term security package. Fringe benefits included a scholarship fund in Michael's name and an annual twelve-day expenses-paid business trip around the world to promote Air Jordan. The deal also featured a clause requiring Nike to spend a million dollars in advertising, and Nike has spent about ten times that since then.

The initial Air Jordan shoes stepped onto the scene shortly before the 1984 NBA season tipped off. The campaign was introduced with a six-city trial that featured the billboards, posters, and the television commercials showing Jordan flying through the air to the background sound of jet engines with his deep voice-over reverberating the slogan "Who said man was not meant to fly?" Since different parts of the shoes were fabricated in Maine, Japan, and Korea, the original supply didn't meet demand. Retailers began tacking premiums onto the price, so if you paid $64.95 for your Air Jordans, or less, you got a deal.

When Jordan first laced up a pair of Air Jordans

for competition, he drew even more attention to himself. And if you've seen the shoes, you know why. The Bulls overreacted because the Air Jordans clashed with the team's red-and-white uniforms. The NBA backed the Bulls, saying that the Air Jordans were against league rules because, as has been established, "They don't have any white in them."

Nike cashed in on the opportunity. They gave Jordan a pair of red, white, and black Air Jordans and produced a new commercial. "On October 15, Nike created a revolutionary new basketball shoe. On October 18, the NBA threw them out of the game. Fortunately, the NBA can't keep you from wearing Air Jordans. By Nike."

The gurus who follow the athletic shoe business believe such a controversy bolstered the success of Air Jordan. Buyers believed that it was the performance factor that led the NBA to ban Air Jordans as if they had some special spring action in the air-insoles. There are those who frequent community centers, gymnasiums, and playgrounds who still believe that is the case.

Falk calls the Jordan effect on endorsements "synergy," which he says is what happens when you add one and one and one and get five. With Jordan it is the way one endorsement leads to another endorsement, and Michael has been overwhelmingly synergistic. Because of the high visibility through Nike, Jordan was even more attractive in the open market. In the advertising business this is known as "rub off," and now Falk could approach a company and sell the idea that other companies were already putting him on television. Wilson Sporting Goods jumped on the bandwagon by paying Jordan $200,000 to put his name on autographed basketballs.

McDonald's wanted to get a piece of Jordan the family man, and, synergistically speaking, that paved the way to a deal with Coke, which is the soft drink McDonald's sells. In its Jordan campaign, Coke has Michael going one-on-one with Max Headroom. The Chicagoland Chevrolet dealers wanted to invest in Jordan's Olympic appeal. But they got a bonus. When Chevy offered Jordan his choice of any car, he picked the Blazer over the sleek Corvette because he figured it would help a boy from the South get around in the winter snow of Chicago. Michael knows what he's doing; he attends every business meeting adorned in a well-tailored suit and carrying a briefcase.

Falk also worked a deal with Johnson products, one of the nation's leading black-owned corporations. Jordan promoted a line of women's hair treatment and Johnson then added a line of men's cosmetic products bearing his name. Falk especially likes this deal because it depicts Jordan as giving something back to the black community. Jordan, however, is one of those rare black athletes who transcends color. Such a trait puts him in the same category as Ashe and O.J. Simpson and satisfies Michael's desire to be perceived as "neither black nor white" in the business world.

He did, however, give something back to his family. When he started Air Jordan Express during the summer of 1987, he named his mother and father as the chief operating officers.

Jordan had stimulated the economy in a way that should make the president of the U.S. and the Congress envious. Within the Chicago Bulls organization he created jobs. "Without putting too much pressure on him," said David Brenner, who moved up from his job in the sales department to become director of promotions when Michael became a Bull, "one guy has changed a lot of lives in this office." As soon as Jordan was drafted, Jonathon Kovler revamped the franchise to prepare for the selling of Michael Jordan.

Kovler put a call into David Rosengard, who at the time was director of marketing for Northwestern University and has since moved on to take charge of operations for the Chicago Sting of the Major Indoor Soccer League. "Jonathon called and said," Rosengard recalled, "I've got Michael Jordan; now what do I do?"

With the start of the season, the Bulls not only unveiled Jordan, but a series of promotions to go with him. On any given night, a fan could venture into the Chicago Stadium and walk out with a poster, a coffee mug, a seat cushion, or a floppy hat, in addition to seeing a great basketball player. Rosengard brought in the Four Tops and the Temptations to do postgame concerts and turn the evening into a double feature. And how did Jordan feel about being the warm-up act for the Temptations? "Well, they've been performing a lot longer than I have."

Life had been pumped into the stadium. Attendance doubled in the first month of the season and season ticket orders continued coming in. "We were lousy last year and lousy the year before that," said ticket manager Joe O'Neil at the time. "Without Jordan we could have lost five hundred more season tickets this year."

With Jordan the Bulls were the hottest ticket in

town. You talk about a return on investment. In his first year, the Bulls paid Michael a salary of $550,000. During that year, home attendance increased 87 percent, and season ticket sales went from $2 million to $3.8 million. And then add in the $190,000 the Bulls received for making the play-offs, something that had not been done in the years before Michael. All totaled, Jordan provided a 350 percent return on investment.

In the years to come, Jordan may command a price to match his market value. The Bulls were so respectful of his propensity to be commercialized that practices were sometimes scheduled around him filming commercials, doing a photo shoot, or making public appearances. But the cost of employing Michael will always be such a deal. He is worth every penny.

9.

A Season on the Brink

MICHAEL JORDAN STEPPED UP TO THE free throw line with 2 seconds left and 2 shots to send this first-round game in the 1986 play-offs at the Boston Garden into overtime. Kevin McHale fouled Jordan on his desperation three-point shot, in the process showing his best impression of a fly swatter, which was the only way to keep up with Michael on this April 20 afternoon. There was, after all, no stopping Jordan, who used every trick in the book and then wrote some of his own chapters in the process of scoring an NBA play-off—record 63 points in the game. The 3-point shot came with the Bulls trailing the Celtics 116–114 and no time left on the clock when McHale came rushing at Jordan with arms flailing because he had tried everything else defensively and failed. Though the shot bounced off the back iron, McHale ran over Jordan, which referee Ed Middleton saw even in the midst of the victory celebration which prematurely erupted in the Garden. And as

Jordan stepped up to the foul line for what would become his 53rd and 54th point in the game, he saw the embittering struggle of the 1986–87 season flash before his eyes.

Michael came into training camp with all the enthusiasm of a rookie. Will he ever grow up? He was excited to prove that last season wasn't a fluke, that the Bulls making the play-offs was the start of many good things to come. Even as the team meandered through an 0–8 preseason in which the Bulls lost the annual game played at Greensboro Coliseum at the University of North Carolina in Chapel Hill, it was apparent things were coming together under new coach Stan Albeck, who had come over from New Jersey to replace Kevin Loughery, who was fired.

Yet Michael seemed almost prophetic in his comments at the end of the exhibition season. Three times he topped the 30-point mark in preseason, enough to make a promise of sorts. "I don't want the Bulls to be in for a long season. I hate long seasons. I want this to be an enjoyable one."

A preview article in one of the Chicago newspapers seemed to serve as another omen: "The joy ride is over for Michael Jordan." But he knew the season would be a different story. He knew expectations would be higher, but he seemed intent on taking the ball to the hole and the Bulls to their goals.

"I may have to score less and pass more this year," he realized. "You may see me with more assists. Maybe I can get more triple-doubles than last year." As Jordan filled the Bulls' Deerfield Multiplex practice facility with his spirit for his sport, he let his teammates know they could count on him for anything and everything if necessary. And more.

"This is where I really have to concentrate this year, to step up and be a leader. I have the respect of all the players now, and if there are things that have to be said, I won't feel out of place."

In the opening game against Cleveland at the Chicago Stadium, Jordan was in the right place at the right time the whole night. He concentrated more on great play making than on making great plays, which helped to set up Woolridge for his team-leading 35 points. Michael added 29 points of his own and hit a free throw with 23 seconds left in overtime to provide the winning margin in a 116–115 victory. When the game was on the line, he scored three straight baskets to give the Bulls a 113–106 lead they were able to hang on to.

By game two, the Bulls were ready to battle. But when Jordan was taken down hard by Detroit's Bill Laimbeer, the NBA's ultimate hatchet man, Albeck came screaming off the bench and eventually got into a pushing and shoving match with Pistons coach Chuck Daly. Jordan eventually wound up squaring off with Isiah Thomas but only within the rules. After the coaches were ejected, this pair of megastars turned the game into a glorified one-on-one and when the final bell—er, buzzer—went off, Michael had scored 33 points and the Bulls had scored a superior decision by a 118–115 count.

With a 111–105 victory over Golden State in Oakland in the third game of the season, the Bulls were undefeated and headed for the top of the league, if not the world. But at the same time the team realized its worst fears. With 45 seconds left in the second quarter, Jordan made a move to his left and jammed. Not the ball, however, but his ankle, the same ankle he hurt during a preseason practice in Houston, and the same one he twisted during the exhibition game in Greensboro. He was carried to the locker room by teammates Charles Oakley and Mike Smrek and taken to a nearby hospital for X rays.

All of a sudden, there was a break in the action. The next day was Halloween and perhaps the scariest day in Michael's life. He hobbled about on crutches nursing his left foot, which was wrapped in a protective brace. X rays were negative, and so was Jordan. Merely walking was a problem, especially for a guy who was used to flying. Here is someone who has never hesitated to play with pain. Before his sophomore season at North Carolina he fractured his wrist, yet he played the first three weeks of the season with his arm heavily bandaged. So when he is talking about missing a game, something must be seriously wrong.

Only Michael could explain what the impact would be. "If I can walk without crutches, I'll try playing," Michael said. "But I don't know what good I am. There is always a chance I could reinjure it. It felt like something popped out of place when I came down flat on my foot, not arched like you usually do to cushion the impact. It was like when a ball comes too fast and it jams your finger."

Then another first came this season. The Bulls lost 120–112 to the Los Angeles Clippers while Michael sat on the bench shouting, encouraging, and pointing his finger because that was all the contribution he could make on this night. As Albeck assessed the game and the impact of not having Jordan, he realized, "It's very difficult to replace 28 points a game." But the talk was still hopeful. "It's going to be nice when we get Michael back out there," Woolridge said.

For now the diagnosis on Michael was, in medical terms, "a severely jammed left ankle." The Bulls lost to Seattle, a team hobbling with its own illnesses, 118–100 for the SuperSonics' first win of the season.

Michael remained hopeful. "I think the team found some confidence they could play without me." But the most prominent common denominator between the past two defeats was Jordan's absence. Something noticeable is missing with Michael not in there. There is a hole where the Bulls' heart should be.

But on the afternoon of November 5, 1985, the broken hearts were overwhelmed by a broken bone —the navicular tarsal bone in Jordan's left foot, to be exact, a fracture that only appeared when a CAT scan, which X-rays bones in layers, was completed. The prognosis was dismal, and the future turned grim. Michael hopefully would miss just six weeks, but to a man who had never been listed as disabled, it seemed like an eternity. And from here to eternity, Michael didn't know what to do to keep himself occupied, let alone sane.

"All I could think of was I would lay up and do nothing. Right now, I can cry all night and wake up tomorrow and find out what it's [the injury] all about." But at this point, there were those who shared Jordan's feeling that there would be no tomorrow.

In the first three games, Jordan had averaged 31 points, 6.5 rebounds, 4.5 assists, and 1.5 blocked shots. Albeck's first reaction was "How do you replace that?" The coach had to redefine roles for his players. Woolridge, Corzine, and newly acquired scoring phenomenon George "Iceman" Gervin would have to pick up the scoring slack. Guards Kyle Macy and John Paxson would have to account for more assists. General manager Jerry Krause scoured the waiver lists to pick up a guard to take Michael's place on the roster and in the backcourt. Obviously, no one man could replace Jordan.

Not to worry, for Bulls trainer Mark Pfeil said the latest he expected Jordan to return was January 2. In the meantime, Michael felt right at home by himself in his Northbrook town house. For a change he had to deal with some privacy. "I'll be all right. Hey, I know how to cook."

With Jordan due for a checkup on his foot in mid-December, all the Bulls were busy making plans accordingly for the holiday season. Albeck checked his list of changes twice. For Jordan, the man who has everything, the coach had presented the idea that he was considering using Michael at small forward instead of big guard. His cast was due to be removed in three days, which was such a gift for Jordan that it didn't matter where he played.

As long as he played. Before a Bulls game on December 23, ticket manager Joe O'Neil saw Jordan sitting on the bench fussing with a basketball, so O'Neil bet Michael ten dollars that he couldn't make one of three shots from his present position on the bench. His face lit up. He flashed a wide-eyed smile, and took the action. After bouncing the first attempt off the back rim, Jordan said, "Now I've got the range." The next shot was a swish; the first one he had made since breaking the bone in his foot. It was getting harder to keep Michael on the bench.

So he went back down to the farm. Not one to waste the opportunity, Jordan returned to Chapel Hill where he spent some time on the Wall, hung out with the home boys, and worked on his conditioning. He even practiced jumping and dunking off his right foot, something he had never done before.

Michael may have been gone, but he was not forgotten. The early returns on voting for the NBA all-star game revealed Jordan keeping pace with Thomas to be in the starting backcourt for the Eastern Conference. Which was right on schedule (we've heard that before) because at a December 27 examination by Bulls team physician Dr. John Hefferon, a CAT scan revealed the navicular tarsal had healed sufficiently to give Jordan a weight-bearing cast to wear for two weeks. At that time, Michael would be examined by two more foot specialists, and on doctor's orders be put in a splint for a week. If all went well, he would "return to the Bulls active roster three weeks from now," Hefferon said, or in other words he would be back by no later than February 1. But we've heard that talk before.

Sure enough, two weeks later Hefferon examined Jordan's foot and learned it was still broken. He put Michael in another walking cast, told him to take two aspirin and call him in another two weeks.

But Michael, as only Michael can, still found a way to contribute to the team. With the Bulls currently running ninth in the race for the Eastern Conference play-offs—only eight teams make it— Jordan addressed the issue at a team meeting. "I told them to start playing some defense," Jordan said. "They were starting to accept defeat. They lose, go home, eat dinner, and start feeling better about losing. I watched the first half of the loss at Detroit the other night, and I was throwing soda cans at the television. This is the first time I've spoken up in a meaningful situation. I've been watching and waiting for the right time to express my feelings without being out of place." Apparently, Michael wanted to be back out on the court in the worst way.

And he was willing to go to great lengths to do so. During a two-day span in February he flew to see Dr. Stanley James in Eugene, Oregon, and to Cleveland to be examined by Dr. John Bergfeld, the Cleveland Browns' team physician. The two doctors hooked up with Jordan, Hefferon, and Bulls management in a conference call that didn't provide what Michael wanted to hear. As a result, he said he would be sitting out four more weeks. But the headline on the sports page of the Chicago Tribune asked what everyone wanted to know: JORDAN LOST FOR THE SEASON?

"I listened to the advice of the three doctors I consulted with," Michael said, "and, in what is an emotional decision, I've decided the best course is not to play until I go through another examination in four weeks."

The next CAT scan revealed that the bone had

healed to the point where Jordan could be ready for the stress of competition. In his mind, it already had, and the only source of stress was not being able to play. Jordan went back to Chapel Hill to work on his college degree and some foul shooting, which eventually became playing in a pickup game four times a week. So much for doctor's orders.

Michael knows best. During rehabilitation sessions with a physical therapist, Jordan was tested on a Cybex, a machine that monitors individual muscle strength, and his left foot proved to be stronger than his right in some cases. According to physical therapist Judy Jaffe, "He was ready to go." With a meeting to discuss his return with Krause and owner Jerry Reinsdorf a few days away, Jordan jumped up and down as if he was preparing for takeoff.

When asked about that meeting to determine how and when Jordan would return, Michael said, "Maybe I should buy them off." Playing time wasn't going to come cheap; Reinsdorf, Krause, and even Falk wanted Michael to sit out the rest of the season. Jordan, however, worked a deal with Reinsdorf and Krause that netted him seven minutes of playing time per game. But Jordan would have sold his soul for this chance. And so it was that on March 15 that Michael's 64-game layoff ended. How soon would Albeck use him? "In warm-ups," the coach said with a laugh.

With 5:59 left in the second quarter of a game against the Milwaukee Bucks, Michael Jordan received a standing ovation as he stripped off his warm-ups and checked into the game. He immediately took the ball right to the basket, and dunked over the Bucks 7-foot-3 center Randy Breuer. He scored 12 points in 12 minutes of play. Everything was OK. The struggle was over.

But a new struggle was just beginning. The more Michael played, the more minutes he wanted each game. In his next outing against the Atlanta Hawks, Michael had to leave with 1:47 left because his allotted playing time had expired. At the time, the Bulls were trailing, 96–88. Before Jordan entered in the second half, the Bulls were down 79–65. They lost 106–96. When Jordan was in during the fourth quarter he made 5 steals, a team record for most steals in a quarter, and scored 13 points in 7 minutes.

But the Bulls still lost, and they were now running tenth in the play-off picture. Jordan contended that his limited playing time was disrupting the team chemistry, and that it was a constant distraction to his concentration. He lashed out at Reinsdorf, saying that he was being kept to a minimum of minutes because the owners didn't want to win. If they didn't make the play-offs, they'd be eligible for the NBA draft lottery, which was a shot at the first pick in the college draft.

Reinsdorf gave into Jordan's request somewhat by upgrading his playing time to 10 minutes a half and promised he would increase it in increments of 2 per game. When he scored 19 points in 19 minutes to spark a victory over the Knicks March 21, the Bulls won for the first time since Michael returned to the lineup five games ago. Even a late-in-the-game plea to Albeck to let him play the rest of a game against the New Jersey Nets resulted in an "I can't" from the coach. The next night he scored 24 points in 23 minutes, including 14 in the fourth quarter to lead the Bulls to a victory over the Knicks in New York. But 28 points in 26 minutes of a loss to the Bucks April 2 did nothing to open management's eyes.

The situation reached ridiculous proportions. When he was taken out of a victory over Indianapolis with 31 seconds left to play because he had reached his limit of 28 minutes, Michael merely said, "If I can play 28 minutes, I'm sure I can play 28 minutes and 31 seconds." He dared to go one minute beyond his limit in the process of scoring 30 points in a 102–97 win over Atlanta and was averaging better than a point a minute since returning to action.

Finally Reinsdorf and Jordan called a press conference to bury the hatchet. The issue was resolved internally. Jordan said, "I have no further comment on that matter," and Reinsdorf added, "I have no further comment on the matter." It wasn't clear who had the last word, but Jordan was content to let his playing do the talking.

April 8 marked Jordan's first start since October 29, 1986, and he scored 10 points in the first quarter as the Bulls opened up a 24–10 lead over Milwaukee and went on to a 107–101 victory that clinched at least a tie for the final spot in the play-offs. Four nights later the Bulls were in the midst of defeating Washington 105–103 to wrap up the play-off spot, and at halftime Reinsdorf, apparently caught up in the moment, waived Jordan's playing time restriction.

The risk appeared to be a good one. Once again there was a great return on investment. Pat Williams, general manager of the Philadelphia 76ers, put it in proper perspective. "What does Michael Jordan mean? He means people in the building. He was good for about 5,000 more a game last year. That's how we view him." By leading the Bulls to the play-offs, he guaranteed an extra $25,000 per player and another $250,000 for the franchise in ticket sales for play-off game three of the opening-round series with the Celtics, which would be played in Chicago.

And though the Bulls were against all odds, Jordan looked on the whole ordeal as a challenge rather than a struggle. "It's similar to when I first went to North Carolina. Nobody wanted me to go there; they all said I would sit on the bench. I went to UNC because it was a challenge. This is similar. No one expects us to win, and we're going to take the challenge."

Jordan provided the unexpected. In the opening game of the play-off he hit his first five shots, and scored over, around, and through the Celtic defense on his way to a 49-point night. Jordan was playing the Celtics 1-on-5 and winning for most of the first half until a last-second shot gave the home team a 61–59 lead. Boston went on to win 123–104, but Jordan's brilliance was the story of this game.

"Want to know how great Jordan is?" Celtics coach K.C. Jones began to explain. "Normally the guys on the bench are leaning forward, trying to make eye contact with me. When they saw what Jordan was doing, nobody wanted to go in. I'd look down the bench, and they were all leaning back. So I leaned back too. When somebody went in, it took so long for their warm-ups to come off."

But Michael was just getting warmed up. In Sunday's second game, Jones could have put the whole team on the floor, and Jordan would have found a way to soar and score. He blew by Bird for a hoop here, then jumped over Dennis Johnson for a basket there. He had 30 points by halftime, and he was getting hotter. A jam, then a scoop lay-up and a 20-foot jump shot, and Michael couldn't miss. When McHale blocked his lane to the basket, Jordan glided under him for a reverse slam. When Danny Ainge tried to stop a drive, Jordan jumped over him for a jam. Finally the score was 116–114 with Boston ahead when Jordan, who had 52 points, put up a 3-point shot and was fouled by McHale as time expired.

Suddenly Woolridge came up behind Jordan on the foul line and slapped him on the butt, which brought Michael back to reality. Here were two free throws that presented a chance to wipe out all the preceding memories. This could be the first day of the rest of the season as far as he was concerned. Michael swished the two free throws, which forced the first overtime. At times, the season seemed like a nightmare, but now he was on the verge of living out another of his dreams. He was the best player in the best game and it was on national television. A victory would perfectly augment the big picture, and then Michael would be able to tell his grandchildren about this afternoon in which he broke the single-game play-off scoring record set by Elgin Baylor on April 14, 1962, before Jordan was ever born. Jordan had a last-second shot in the first overtime to win the game, but he missed. The Bulls eventually lost 135–131 in double overtime. Judging by the course of events that overshadowed this season, perhaps it just wasn't meant to be.

But even as the Bulls dropped the next game to lose the series, 3–0, the rave reviews over Jordan's miraculous performance continued to surface. The ultimate conclusion was that no one would ever do anything like that again. But where Michael is concerned, we've all heard that before.

10.

A Bird's-Eye View

LARRY BIRD SAT IN HIS DRESSING CUBICLE in the Celtics locker room at Boston Garden shaking his head. He had just witnessed vintage Jordan as he soared to his 63 points, and Bird's eye view that afternoon consisted mainly of looking up right into the soles of Michael's Air Jordans. But good old Larry Bird merely stared right back at his questioners as if to ask, "Who said man was not meant to fly?" Naturally Bird, who has been the subject of numerous compliments, had plenty to say about Jordan's feat of that afternoon. And this was no small talk, which players sometimes pass off because that's what everybody else wants to hear. Bird had no problem running off at the mouth after being party to what was already being called one of the most amazing performances in the history of the game.

"I couldn't believe anybody could do that against the Boston Celtics," Bird said. "[Michael] had to have one of the greatest feelings you can

North Carolina teammate Matt Doherty starts the celebration, and all eyes are fixed on Michael as he finishes off a cradle jam and another Tar Heel victory over Clemson. (Photo courtesy of Chapel Hill Newspaper)

Michael takes a breather and refuels during a Carolina game. (Photo courtesy of Chapel Hill Newspaper)

Even at North Carolina, Michael was making moves which were hard to believe. Villanova's Ed Pinckney (#54) and Dwayne McClain (#33) find it hard to believe as well. (Photo courtesy of Chapel Hill Newspaper)

Even a pack of Rutgers players can't keep Carolina's Jordan from taking off and dishing off. (Photo courtesy of Chapel Hill Newspaper)

With his tongue in proper position, Michael apparently is setting himself for lift-off on a baseline drive to the hoop. (Photo courtesy of Chapel Hill Newspaper)

Jordan defies all rules of verticality, not to mention gravity. (Photo courtesy of Chapel Hill Newspaper)

Michael hangs on a fadeaway J. over Wake Forest's Anthony Teachey. (Photo courtesy of Chapel Hill Newspaper)

Michael demonstrates the shooting form which enables him to put the ball in the basket so proficiently. (Photo courtesy University of North Carolina Sports Information Department)

Jordan puts down a two-hand jam as his contribution to the Olympic effort. He was the captain of the 1984 team which won the gold medal in Los Angeles. (Photo courtesy of Chapel Hill Newspaper)

Jordan uses everything he has to drive past Jeff Malone of the Washington Bullets. (Peter Mitchell)

Charles Oakley sets a pick for Michael as he maneuvers for a jump shot in a game against Washington. (Peter Mitchell)

Jordan has that ability to rise above a crowd of defenders and score. (Peter Mitchell)

All 7-foot-6 of Washington's Manute Bol can't keep Jordan from gliding under the hoop to a reverse lay-up. (Peter Mitchell)

Sometimes Michael can't believe he does what he does when he winds up with a one-handed jam. (Jonathan Daniel)

Michael also skies when he goes up for rebounds, and on this play he pulls one away from Milwaukee's Paul Pressey. (Jonathan Daniel)

Jordan is the type of player who looks past his defender when he's looking to score. (Jonathan Daniel)

Hanging on the rim is often the best way for Jordan to secure a safe landing after a cradle jam. (Jonathan Daniel)

Michael spends many hours working to get his shooting form perfect. Keeping the ball up high is one of the secrets to the success of his potent jump shot. (Jonathan Daniel)

When Michael gets near the rim and another dunk is on hand, his eyes always seem to light up. (Jonathan Daniel)

The thing about Jordan is that he always manages to get off a shot whether he's falling or sprawling. (Jonathan Daniel)

Sometimes it seems like Michael can squeeze the air out of the basketball then jam it through the hole. Actually, when he has the ball in his hands, he has the game in hand. (Jonathan Daniel)

ever have. No question he had control of the game. It shows you what kind of person he is. I think he's God disguised as Michael Jordan."

Word is out about Michael Jordan; he is the most talked about player in the National Basketball Association. Okay, talk may be cheap, but only because there is so much of it about Michael. It is more than just hear-say. Words usually don't do justice to Jordan, unless it's the people who have played and coached against him who are doing the talking. The best view of Jordan seems to come from watching him blow by you for a superlative slam, or being there on the sideline when he works his magic down the stretch to beat your team. We're not talking trash here.

What hasn't been said already about Michael? What more can be said after Tom Newell called him "the one phenomenon in basketball?" So far we know that Bobby Knight has said, "He is a player," and that Antonio Diaz-Miguel, the coach of the Spanish Olympic team, described him as a "rubber man." George Raveling, the assistant coach of the U.S. Olympic team in 1984, submitted, "In two or three years, there will be a major controversy in the NBA. It will concern how Michael Jordan was allowed to be drafted only third instead of first or second." Don Nelson had told us, "We tried a double-team on him, and he just jumped right over it." Just recently Philadelphia 76ers general manager Pat Williams declared, "Michael means people in the stadium." According to Johnny Dawkins, who guarded Jordan more times than he cares to remember when both of them were in college, Michael beats an opponent in so many ways, but most of all, "He outthinks you."

But even 1,000 words may not begin to describe the big picture, which most opponents perceive as Jordan. Those players who have had the misfortune of guarding Jordan share an up-close, personal view and have put that perspective in their own words. The coaches who have spent long hours creating ways to stop Michael have another story to tell. Of course, sometimes you have to defer to the rest of the players to get the word on Michael. But realize that none of the chatter is exaggeration. Believe it, for as former teammate Sidney Green said and former teammate Caldwell Jones confirmed, "He is the truth, the whole truth, and nothing but the truth."

Basketball coaches are an interesting lot. At times, they may stretch the truth if it's for the good of the cause, or at least the good of the team. In good moods you can't shut them up, but when times are tough they have very little to say. Some will answer questions with a joke and a smile, while others like to quote right from the book of coaches' clichés. But when the topic of conversation is Jordan, the coaches deliver nothing but straight talk.

Don Nelson has provided a complete dissertation about Jordan in the three short years he spent with the Milwaukee Bucks coaching against him. His best quips seemed to be spurred by Jordan's best moments. After watching Michael score 28 points in 26 minutes, Nelson said Jordan was "superhuman." The coach continued, "I don't like to play against him. But the NBA needs him, and it's a great addition to any game to see him play." Finally, after Jordan wreaked havoc on the Bucks during the 1985 season when he was in the process of rehabilitating his foot and still on limited playing time, Nelson called over to Bulls coach Stan Albeck late in the fourth quarter to remind him, "Michael's seven minutes are up."

Albeck never hesitated to accord words of praise to Michael, but even before he coached the Bulls he had good things to say. After Jordan scored 27 points and dished out 7 assists in leading the Bulls to 100–94 win over Albeck and his New Jersey Nets, the coach was all talk. "Michael Jordan is not only a great scorer, he is also a great passer," Albeck began. "He has unbelievable hang time. He can stay up there, jump over the double-team, and then have the innate ability to get the ball to the open man no matter where he is on the floor. That part of him isn't talked about enough."

Maybe it's Michael's former coaches who have the best point of view. Once you've seen him do it for you, you hate to see him do it to you. Kevin Loughery was coaching the Washington Bullets in 1986 when Jordan came to town and promptly hit just 9-of-25 shots from the field against what seemed to be a defense created just to hold him down. Yet stopping Jordan sometimes isn't even stopping Jordan, and after he scored 28 points in the game, Loughery knew just what to say. "Well, having coached him didn't give me any expertise on stopping him," said Loughery, whom Jordan credits as being the coach who did the most to make him the player that he is today. "You don't stop Michael Jordan unless you double- and triple-team him. Michael Jordan is maybe the best 6-6 guy ever to play the game. I think Michael is going to see a lot of double- and triple-teams, and the decision will be who else is going to beat you? Oh, he's such a great player [even with double- and triple-teaming] he can still beat you."

Even when he doesn't beat them, coaches still find time to drop a line about Jordan. But after he scored 38 points and added 12 rebounds and 7 assists in a 110–107 loss to Indiana on January 21, 1985, Pacers coach George Irvine was almost at a loss for words. "I can't believe it," Irvine exclaimed. "Michael Jordan is something else. You have to change your defense completely [against him]. He just keeps getting better. Tonight he had to earn his points, but he did it."

And the beat rambles on. After Jordan scored 14 points in 7 minutes of the fourth quarter to nearly salvage a victory in Atlanta, Hawks coach Mike Fratello could have rambled on about Jordan all night. These were words to live by: "Nothing Michael Jordan does surprises me," Fratello reiterated, "nothing. He is one of the greatest players I've ever seen play. He is such a pivotal player for the Bulls in so many ways. He walks out on the floor, and the first thing he does is swipe two balls. That's two steals and two baskets. He does that incredible reverse move under the basket, misses, gets his own rebound and scores a 3-point play."

It seems they can't say enough. Notice that when it comes to speaking on this subject, they always refer to him as "Michael Jordan," as if using the first name and the surname is the sign of the utmost respect. And they always talk in specifics. Jordan is the type of player who makes such memorable moves, coaches and players have no trouble recalling them when the game is over. And you'll notice there is never a bad word.

Perhaps some talk in terms of frustration. "There

is no sense stopping Jordan if he can get the ball to the other guys who score inside," said Denver coach Doug Moe after his team suffered a 122–113 loss to the Bulls in which Jordan had a triple-double. "Jordan was just spectacular."

And there even have been words of consolation. When Michael suffered through a dismal afternoon in his first NBA all-star game, Boston's K.C. Jones, who was coaching the Eastern Conference all-stars, had no trouble voicing a favorable opinion of Jordan. "There's a whole lot of talent out there, the greatest players in the game," Jones said. "Michael will be one and is one. But it's not easy. It's a measure of the man that he didn't try to force things." When Jordan scored 41 points, grabbed 12 rebounds, and almost beat the Celtics with a last-second shot, Jones had an alternative point of view. "All I can think of is that quote, 'Air Jordan.' He is utterly awesome."

The NBA's executives have made it a point to stick in their two sense. "Michael Jordan should be declared a national treasure," said Bill Needle, public relations director of the Atlanta Hawks. "There is no question he is absolutely the greatest drawing card in the league," added Harvey Kirkpatrick, the Denver Nuggets' communications director. NBA spokesman Terry Lyons had more to say about that notion: "Listing guys you go and put your money down to see, he's got to be number one. I'm sure people in Boston might disagree, but when you list all those great players—Bird, Magic Johnson, Charles Barkley, Julius Erving—Michael Jordan is the people's choice." Harvey Shank, director of marketing for the Phoenix Suns, had some last words to add: "Michael Jordan is in a class by himself. Michael Jordan coming to town is like a major entertainer appearing in Phoenix. To the basketball fan, he is Bruce Springsteen. People line up outside the locker room before warm-ups just to get a glimpse of him. As soon as he passes by, they surge back to their seats to watch him warm up."

To know Jordan, however, is to guard him. On the playground, defending a player is known as "holding" him as in "holding him down." But where Michael is concerned, the term has come to mean no holds barred. Some players have made a science of holding Jordan, others have made a career of it. Michael Cooper of the Lakers and Sidney Moncrief of the Bucks are the perennial defensive players of the year in the NBA, but each has barely managed to hold his own against Michael. Moncrief's first attempt came in the third exhibition game of Jordan's rookie season, when El Sid "held" Michael to 22 points. That's the best Moncrief has done against Jordan since.

Michael was seemingly out of reach of the best defensive players in the league early in his rookie season, but then he ran into Denver's T.R. Dunn. Prior to the game, the Denver media had billed this matchup as a duel of sorts, a shoot-out in the Mile High City. But Michael couldn't shoot over T.R., nor could he drive around Dunn. Jordan scored a season-low 17 points, and as Dunn slumped in front of his locker after the game, it was apparent he didn't hold anything back in stopping Jordan. Dunn seemed so tired he didn't want to talk about it, but he did. "Playing Michael Jordan takes an awful lot out of you. Being aware of where he is and keeping the ball away from him is very demanding. We had everybody on the team aware of where he was on the floor at all times. He demands that kind of attention. Because he is so talented, every team he plays is going to be aware of him."

But what's it like to bend way down, grab your shorts, and suck it up to play defense on Michael one-on-one? "When Michael gets that ball and comes down and looks you in the eye, you know something is going to happen," said Rick Carlisle, who squared off with Michael while with the Boston Celtics and while playing college ball in the ACC for the University of Virginia. "The only good thing that can happen is that he misses a shot or they aren't ready for one of his passes. When he looks me in the eye, I try to look at his stomach. It's the only part of him that doesn't move."

Glenn Rivers of the Atlanta Hawks shared a Bird's-eye view when he was a step behind Jordan as he scored 33 points. "Man, Michael Jordan is a great player. He doesn't need any help from the refs. For me, he is the hardest guy to hold in the NBA. It's hard enough already trying to slow him down." But Indiana's Vern Fleming, who guarded Jordan during the Olympic Trials in 1984, realizes sometimes it can be an exercise in futility. "I try to make him work for his shots, shoot his jump shot. If those are going down, you're in for a long night." When it comes to holding Jordan, though, it may have been the Celtics Danny Ainge who said it best: "Nobody can stop Michael Jordan."

As the legend goes, the last guy to stop Michael Jordan was Dan Dakich, who held Jordan to 13 points when Indiana—the University—defeated North Carolina in the 1984 NCAA Tournament.

What makes the moment so memorable was the way it happened. "I remember when I was told I'd be the guy guarding him in that game," Dakich said. "I went back to my dorm room and threw up." Even when he was in college, opponents perceived Michael as something special, and they couldn't stop talking about him. Said Mark Alarie of Duke: "Even though he is the most talented, Michael works harder on the court in every game. That's the unique aspect about him." Bruce Dalyrymple of Georgia Tech offered a second opinion: "Incredible worker with an incredible amount of talent. That combination makes Jordan so great. His attitude is: You can push me or hit me, but I'm going to do what has to be done. It shows in his face. When Michael gets excited, the entire team gets going."

To be sure, Jordan has been the topic of conversation in many an opposing locker room. The things his peers have to say about him might imply that Jordan is peerless. But these guys know what they're talking about.

"The name of the game is to force a player to do the one thing he can't do real well," said 7'2" center Artis Gilmore when he was with the San Antonio Spurs. "But as far as I can tell, Jordan doesn't have that one thing."

"And when the money is on the line," says San Antonio's Alvin Robertson, "you can see him change, see it in his face."

"He'll probably be one of the guys who invents a new position," says the Pistons Isiah Thomas. After seeing a Jordan slam come down in his face, Michael Holton of the Phoenix Suns provided a unique point of view: "All I saw were the bottoms of his shoes." San Antonio's Johnny Moore put it in a language all his own: "He's got talent, and he's got the blue light. That's even better than the green light." The Celtics Dennis Johnson simply says of Jordan, "He's a step above the rest. I read a little program insert or something that said he could have been a great athlete in any sport he chose to play. Well, I believe it. And I wish he'd chosen some other sport."

Wait, it gets better. When Dominique Wilkins and Jordan turned a Bulls–Atlanta game into their personal dunk-fest, Wilkins didn't wait to until after the game to talk about how he outslammed Michael 57 points to 41 points. "He would come up the court, and make an unbelievable move," Wilkins said, "and I would compliment him. I would go back down and do the same, and he would compliment me. When you play against Michael Jordan, you play against the best. He is the toughest athlete I have played against, no question." Added Atlanta guard Glenn Rivers about that night, "I wish I could have been in the crowd just to watch the game."

But the last word should be accorded to a man the stature of Bird. He is clearly the elder statesman in the NBA, the player the reporters flock to for the last word on just about anything. Perhaps it's because Bird has been on the receiving end of so many of Jordan's greatest games, that he has formed such a credible opinion. When Jordan scored 41 points in a loss to the Celtics in the Chicago Stadium during Michael's rookie season, Bird was all talk.

"I've never seen one player turn a team around like that," he said while snapping his fingers.

"Pretty soon, this place will be packed every night, not just when the Celtics come to town. They'll pay just to watch Jordan. He's the best. At this stage in his career, he's doing more than I did. I couldn't do what he did as a rookie. Heck, there was one drive tonight—he had the ball up in his right hand, then he brought it down, then he brought it back up. I fouled him, and he still scored. All the while he's in the air. You have to play this game to know how difficult that is. I thought he was good, but not this good. Ain't nothing he can't do. Never seen anyone like him. Phenomenal. One of a kind."

Bird said it all.

11.

Come Fly with Me

THERE IS A MOMENT THAT CAN OCCUR ANY given time you watch Michael in the midst of his midair magic. Rows of people, whether it be in the stadium or in the living room, see Jordan take off and perform his sleight of hand, then start shaking their heads and wondering, "How'd he do that?"

How does he do it? What's it like to float through the air with the greatest of ease? Why does he do it? Why is he always sticking out his tongue at us? What is it that makes Michael feel playing hurt is better than not playing at all? Why does he pay whatever the price to win? Does he have to win at all costs, or does he work hard and play hard because he hates to lose?

Only Michael himself can provide the answers from his usual position somewhere high above the rim. And everyone is curious to know what the view is like from the top. But Michael has no secrets; when he's soaring and scoring, he'd just as soon take everyone along for the ride. So he talks about how he does what he does, because that is his way of saying come fly with me.

"Sometimes I think about how high I get up," says Jordan of his depth-defying leaps. "I always spread my legs when I jump high, like my rock-a-baby, and it seems like I've opened a parachute, like that slowly brings me back to the floor."

While Jordan cannot fully explain what transpires once he leaves the floor, in everything else he does, he has his feet firmly on the ground. Michael endorses the theory that the way you dress says a lot about the man, and he has a lot to say about the way he dresses on the court. The omnipresent wristband—white at home, red for away—is pushed halfway up his left forearm in memorandum. It serves no other purpose now than to give fanatic imitators an obvious way to duplicate Jordan's look. But he started wearing a wristband in such a position when he was a sophomore at North Carolina in memory of Buzz Peterson, who injured his knee and missed that 1982–83 season. By the way, if you have noticed, he laces up his Air Jordans to the second eyelet from the top for a much simpler reason: "I've always done it that way."

But what really complements the complete Jordan look is the way he wears his shorts. Like everyone else, he puts them on one leg at a time but these shorts seem to be perfect for Michael because they are larger than life. No one except Jordan could fill shorts that big, and if he takes off and catches a draft of air under those baggy pants, it just might enhance his hang time. Actually, though, they are a crutch for Michael, and when he's bending over to catch a breather he grabs them. Or when he gets down and prepares to move his feet on defense, he grabs his shorts as if to dig in and brace himself. Sizing up the situation, Jordan says, "I used to wear 36's, but now I'm into 34's, and they're two inches longer than normal."

Since duplication is the sincerest form of flattery, Nike may want to sell Air Jordan oversized shorts, and perhaps wristbands that fit best when worn halfway up the forearm. But only an ice cream company and the U.S. Postal Service could cash in on Jordan's most copied characteristic. Even with the wristband and the shorts, you can't properly imitate Jordan without a protruding tongue. Indeed, Michael has made sticking out your tongue acceptable, even fashionable again. He, however, is the only adult who can get away with it.

"My father used to have his tongue out when he'd be working on the car, doing mechanical stuff," says Jordan of the origin of his tongue-in-cheek style. It's not a conscious thing. I can't play with it in."

When Michael was at North Carolina, coach Dean Smith wanted to have a mouthpiece made to protect Jordan's tongue, but he couldn't wear one and talk on defense at the same time. And now that America's youth think extending the tongue is the secret to flying, Jordan too is worried. "I'm afraid they might bite them off. For your tongue's sake, kids, don't do it."

Michael may be often imitated, but never duplicated, because not even he is sure how he creates his flight patterns. Everyone has a different favorite dunk because no two of Jordan's slams are the same. The longer he hangs, the more people get a bang out of it, but there are times when even

Michael wishes he had "that" move on film so he could see it again. He's not exactly sure how high he gets up because "I've never had my vertical leap measured." And he'd love to tell us exactly how he does it, but when he reaches the point of takeoff even Michael loses his head. The best we can do is look at things as he sees them.

"I go up for a normal shot, but after that I don't have any plans. I never practice those moves. I don't know how I do them. It's amazing. I wish I could show you a film of a dunk I had in Milwaukee. It looks like I'm taking off, like somebody put wings on me. I get chills when I see it. Sometimes I think, when does 'jump' become 'flying.'"

There is a formula for Michael's ability nonpareil. This package features unsurpassed quickness, incredible jumping, leaping, and hanging ability, each of which is a separate entity. But with that natural talent, Jordan is a tireless worker, which is probably what really sets him above the rest. Mix in a pure hatred for losing and a desire to play despite the utmost pain, and that is what Michael himself might call "the secret of my success."

Jordan stays one step ahead of his defender with his quickness. He looks at his man as a means of setting him up. Then he fakes left and sticks out his tongue as if to say, "Here I go." *Bang.* In one giant drop step he is on his way to the rim. That first step is so quick, so explosive, many officials have whistled him for traveling because they don't think moving that fast is possible. Or legal. "I don't know if his first step is legal," said Jim Thomas, who used to play for the Indiana Pacers, "because I've never had time to judge it."

Before Jordan, jumping was nothing so technical.

You either jumped or you didn't. But if a player manages to stay with Jordan step-for-step, he can outjump a player in different ways. "Larry Nance jumps well off one foot, and Orlando Woolridge jumps well off two," said former Bull Rod Higgins. "Michael jumps well off one or two."

Jumping with him won't necessarily get the job done, however, because Michael can glide. Clearly, he has presented a new outlook to the concept of hanging around. Before Jordan, hang time was something for measuring punts in football or the amount of time one spends down on the corner with the home boys. When Jordan first took off, though, it was possible to put a clock on his flight time. "He has more hang time than [former NFL punter] Ray Guy," said Fred Carter, an assistant coach with the Bulls during the 1986–87 season. And then there is his magic touch. No matter where he is in the air, Michael can will the ball into the basket from wherever he shoots, or so it seems. "The really amazing thing," says Knicks Darrell Walker, "is that when he gets his shot off, it's so soft."

Sometimes Michael can rely completely on his will to score. He talks to his defender—nothing cocky or arrogant but just jawin' as part of the game. James Jordan has seen this innate ability in his son for a long time now, and he noticed it at its best when Michael scored 50 points against the Knicks in the opening game of the 1986–87 season. "Michael talked to Rory Sparrow the whole game," James recalls. "Sparrow was asking, 'Which way you going, Michael?' and Michael's saying 'I'm going left.' And he'd fake right and go left, and Rory would shake his head. It kept happening. 'What you gonna do, Michael?' And Michael would tell him, 'I'm gonna go right' or 'I'm gonna go baseline; better stop me.' And he'd fake him and then do exactly what he said. It's natural. That's the competitive edge coming out of him, saying, 'Don't think you can stop me if I really want to do it.'"

When Michael makes his mind up to do something, clearly there's no changing it, which means he's going to play hurt because that is better than not playing at all. His work habits are an inspiration to all who know of him, but what is it that has inspired Jordan to work so tirelessly on perfecting his game?

Details of the extremes he goes to are well documented. During the three-practices-a-day, give-me-liniment-or-give-me-death workouts that went with being a member of the 1984 Olympic team, Jordan's teammates would prepare for the final session, then sit on the court until Coach Knight appeared. Michael, though, would always be the one still standing, "working on his 360 dunks or something," remembers Olympian Chris Mullin. "I'm watching him, and I realize I'm gonna have to guard him once practice starts. Why me?"

Jordan's affinity for hard work prompts most ignorant bystanders to shake their heads. Perhaps such a quality is something that has resulted from Michael's blue-collar roots. We're talking about someone who comes into the NBA and in a few short weeks is the league's once-in-a-lifetime sensation. Yet all he has to say about the whole ordeal is, "I'm working on my defense. Defensive consistency is my number-one goal."

Michael first acquired the feeling when he was a

sophomore at Laney. It was the most disappointing time in his life, perhaps, when he wasn't promoted to the varsity team his sophomore year after having a wonderful junior varsity season. After that incident (for more details page back to Chapter Two), Jordan dedicated himself to the game. He worked on basketball like he never had before.

"I really started to become a gym rat," he recalls. "I played all the time during that summer, every day. That's when I gave up football. I didn't even play baseball too much that summer."

Nowadays, summer is the only time Michael takes off from playing, but he still has that "love-of-the-game" clause in his contract that permits him to play whenever he wants without permission from the Bulls. It's not uncommon for Jordan to venture to the park across the street from his Northbrook town house for an hour or so on a hot summer day if he feels his jump shot needs a little work.

Just ask Michael and he'll say there is always work to be done. During his season on the brink, Albeck was planning to play Jordan at small forward once he regained his health and returned to full strength. Though Jordan hadn't played much inside in his career, his response to the idea was simple: "I could learn." After his rookie season, he promptly went to work on his passing and ball handling because he knew more adeptness in those areas might lead the Bulls to more victories. And during that rookie season, when the team was floundering even though Michael was doing everything in his power, he offered to work harder on his rebounding because he thought that would inspire his teammates to do the same.

What Michael goes through to play this game is awe-inspiring. He would be walking on crutches during a practice sometimes because his ankle was so severely sprained, but if there was a game the next day, he'd say, "Well, if I can walk on it, I'll play." The doctors might tell him, "Walk, don't jump," but he'd be out on the court, because playing in pain means he's not playing in vain. The morning the navicular tarsal bone in his left foot was first diagnosed as broken in 1985, Jordan was shooting around at practice trying to convince himself he was getting better. Even when his coaches and attorneys have questioned Jordan's decisions to play with injuries, there has never been a doubt in his mind. Don't ever question Michael's sanity, for some of his greatest performances have come while nursing a bad ankle, back, or finger.

There is a theory that playing in pain can improve one's concentration on the court. Magic Johnson had the best year of his career in 1986–87, even though he was playing on knees so sore there were days when he could barely walk. Jordan is one of those players who picks his game up a notch when injuries are nagging him. He overcomes pain like he overcomes a nagging opponent.

"I'm a competitive person, and I want to play," he said after scoring 21 points on a bad ankle against the Knicks on December 8, 1984. "Sure I listen to the doctor. It's his opinion, but it's still my choice." In that very game, it was Jordan who overcame a twisted ankle in the third quarter and a double-team in the waning moments to hit a 20-foot jump shot at the buzzer and give the Bulls a 95–93 victory. "I just laced up my shoes a little tighter and continued to play. I didn't feel the pain on the last shot."

On a night when Jordan swished a jumper with 53 seconds left to bring the Bulls to within 2 points of the Celtics 99–97, who would have figured Michael spent that entire day in bed with the flu? And even though he scored 30 points in 11-of-17 shooting from the field, in the end Jordan's source of discomfort was the 105–97 loss rather than a fever. It's as if Michael plays for medicinal purposes. When he scored 34 points, pulled down 8 rebounds, and dished out 7 assists to lead the Bulls to a 132–129 victory over Atlanta in double overtime, Jordan sat at his locker afterward wearing a weary expression and revealed that he played with an extremely sore back. "I must be getting old," he joked. "My back was really bothering me, and I had to push it. But now it feels pretty good."

Remember, he was the one who told everybody involved—agents, owners, coaches, doctors, general managers—the best rehabilitation for his broken foot was to play. Doctors may give the orders, but Michael feels he knows best. "I've got to try it out and see what happens," he said at the time. "Let's say I sit out the rest of the season, and then I go to training camp and reinjure it. Now, I'm going to mess up another year. This way, if it's not completely ready, I'll find out and I'll have the entire off-season to let it heal."

Sometimes with Jordan, you don't know he's hurting until he comes out of practice the day after the game with his thumb in an ace bandage or ice on his hip. His obsessive competitiveness makes Michael do what's best for the good of the cause first and foremost. In a 93–76 win over Seattle on

January 25, 1985, Jordan suffered a sprained ankle midway through the third quarter and still managed 22 points and 8 assists. His foot may have been hurt, but not his pride. "It's sore enough to make me limp, but it'll be better tomorrow. I plan on playing. Do you think anyone is going to keep me away from the game tomorrow night?"

He came back the next night to score 45 points with 10 assists, 8 rebounds, and 4 blocked shots in leading the Bulls to a 117–104 win over Atlanta. He hit his first 9 shots of the contest, when the intensity of the game apparently made him numb to the pain. "I felt great during the game, and even now it feels okay. I can walk normal," Michael said. Added coach Kevin Loughery, "Michael played after getting treatment for his ankle early this morning and right before the game. This game is a tribute to Michael."

Jordan's will to win is a tribute to the game. There is no question Michael would trade every one of the 63 points he scored that afternoon in the Boston Garden for the victory. Hitting the shot to win the national championship in 1981 was important to Michael not because he made the shot, but because Carolina won the game. These days when he's not practicing or playing hoops, he's involved in a card game or a game of pool or out on the golf course trying to beat someone or some thing. And above everything else, it could be his compulsion to win that is the fuel that sends Air Jordan flying. Next time you see Michael play, watch him at the end of the game. His eyes get wider, his tongue hangs out farther; it's as if he has an overdrive gear he shifts into when the victory is there for the taking because, says James Jordan, "Michael hates to lose at anything." Whether it's the last-second shot against the Knicks or against Georgetown, you want the ball in Jordan's hands because he's going to find some way to get it in the basket.

If there was one thing that gave Michael hope when he was growing up, it was winning. Early on, life always meant one more one-on-one with Larry so Michael could get one last shot at winning. He was always the one in the neighborhood organizing the games, for without any games there would be no opportunity to win. This is one of James Jordan's most vivid memories. "Michael has always been very competitive.

"I can remember the kids always gathering in our yard to play ball. You know how it is. When there's a group with not enough kids, and you don't have a rule book, they make up the rules as they go. But not Michael; he wanted to play by the rules. That way, he could know how to win and who the winner would be. He always wanted to be the best."

He still does. Jordan took up the game of golf toward the end of his days at Carolina, and the game is supposed to be good for relaxation. Originally, that was enough, but now Michael wants to be the best golfer. He even talks about how when his days in the NBA are finished, he'd like to join the professional golf tour. The thing is, though, he'll probably do it.

His will to win is legendary. Even in college, Jordan wouldn't take even the possibility of losing lying down. "If he's lying in bed ready to go to sleep and you tell him you can beat him in pool, he'll get up, go downstairs, and play until he proves you wrong," said Brad Daugherty, one of Michael's

Carolina teammates. "You can't tell Michael you can beat him at something. He won't accept it."

Peterson is the man who has all the goods on Jordan, having stayed up many a night playing everything from gin rummy to Trivial Pursuit with his roommate. But there is one story Buzz loves to tell that really describes this quality in Jordan. As Peterson recalls, one time the two of them and their dates went head-to-head in what became an intense game of Monopoly. But when it became evident that Buzz and his date were going to get the upper hand this time, Jordan threw his money at his opponents and stormed out of the room. Embarrassed? Humiliated? Beaten? "I stayed with my sister that night," Michael said. "I just couldn't face Buzz."

If there is one thing Michael has trouble dealing with, it's defeat. You can see it on the court. He doesn't provide resounding dunks and surprising steals when the Bulls are being blown out because the show must go on. Jordan is the type of player who does whatever he can to win until the final buzzer sounds. If it's a lost cause, Jordan will answer all questions by putting the blame on himself. But then, the Bulls go and beat Portland on January 22, 1985, for the team's third victory in a row; Jordan scores 25 points in the game, and he's all talk afterward. "This is the type of game we have to play every night," he says, all the while getting more excited with each word. "That's the feeling right now. We have a chance to win four in a row. We've got a chance to break that stretch of winning one and losing one."

Make no mistake, though, for Michael is a winner with every move he makes, every breath he takes.

As Matt Doherty said, "That is the string that ties the whole package together." When he was making his comeback off the broken foot, Jordan seemed to be getting better with every minute he played. But since his return to the lineup, the team had lost five straight games, and how well he was playing was unimportant to him. "I was disrupting the chemistry of the team. What else can I think? They had won three in a row, and since I've been back, they haven't won a game." Can you imagine? The guy was scoring a point a minute since his return, and because the team wasn't winning, he was taking the blame.

To win or how to win, that is the question for Michael. He'll invite a guest into his home, lead him to the pool table, and then begin to sink shot after shot. "Uh huh," he says, "the house wins. The house always wins."

No question about it.

12.

A Flight to Remember

MICHAEL LISTENED TO THE ROAR OF THE capacity crowd rocking the Seattle Kingdome in anticipation of his next sky ride in the 1987 NBA Slam-Dunk Competition. He knew what they wanted. So Jordan started backpedaling from one end of the court toward the opposite baseline, and with each step a flush came over the crowd. Michael reached his destination, then prepared for the flight by coiling his body like a rubber band tightening on a windup toy plane. He headed down the court as if it were a runway, accelerated to full speed, and picked up momentum as he crossed midcourt. And as he catapulted off the free-throw line to complete a rousing double-pump slam, Jordan not only transcended gravity but time as well. It was this very dunk Julius Erving premiered in 1976 when he won the American Basketball Association's inaugural slam-dunk contest, an event that more than any other started the art of jamming on the path to its current status. Even as Jordan soared to become the best of the best dunkers in the 1987 competition, he realized, "It all goes back to Doc. That's where the dunks come from. I added a little with the pump, but the roots started with Dr. J."

If dunking does indeed have a family tree, then it's Doc Erving who is the forefather. And if he is the first generation, then Jordan certainly is the dawning of the next generation. Dominique Wilkins and Larry Nance are perhaps branches of this tree, but it's Erving who first planted the idea that dunking is the single most crowd-pleasing moment in all of sport. And it's Jordan who has helped such a feeling grow to the point where the best jammers have to gather once a year to strut their best stuffs. It was Erving who first displayed the unforeseen athletic ability the gurus of the game saw in Jordan and called sky-walking. If it was Erving who created the rule of verticality—which entitles a player to the airspace above him—it was Jordan who took such an entity to new heights and invented hang time. The gurus of the game used to sit around and tell stories about Erving's suspended animation, but now they just sit back and shake their heads over Michael's feats. And when Michael completed the last of his hang gliding to win the 1987 NBA slam-dunk contest, clearly it was time to move over, Dr. J., and make room for Dr. Jordan.

Jordan and Erving first faced each other face-to-face when the Bulls first played Philadelphia in November of 1984, Jordan's rookie season. It was a summit that had all the impact of Lee meeting

Grant at Appomattox, Reagan meeting Gorbachov, or perhaps David meeting Goliath. They stood at midcourt and gave each other the once-over. The conversation was congenial, even friendly, filled with the personality that also has set these two head and shoulders above the rest. "I told him I thought he was taller," Erving said. "He told me he thought I was taller too."

It may be no coincidence that there is a lot of Erving in Jordan. Both love to play to the crowd. Fans were rushing to the 76ers basket to watch Erving do his dunking during warm-ups, while Jordan was still creating his repertoire on the outdoor court at Trask Junior High in Wilmington. When Julius went up in the air the crowd stood up to watch. Michael says that when he's in the open and closing in on the rim he thinks of "ways that will excite the crowd." Both players are talked about and talked to in the same regard. Erving has long been considered the best interview in the NBA with his intelligent, outgoing, often humorous nature. He was the elder statesman in the league, the classiest player around. Jordan was voted to the NBA's all-interview team in 1987, and because of his gentle sense of humor, engaging smile, and mature presence, former Bulls general manager Rod Thorn calls him a "class act."

While comparing and contrasting Erving and Jordan makes for stimulating barroom and/or courtyard conversation, it's "not fair to Michael Jordan or to Julius Erving," Jordan says. Even Kevin Loughery, who coached Erving during the height of his career in the ABA and Jordan, declines to make a clear-cut comparison. "They even know who Doc is in Russia," Loughery says, "It's hard in this day and age of athletics to compare anyone to Julius on or off the court. He was unbelievable for an athlete of his stature, the way he handled people and situations. No one else is even close. But Michael plays with an awful lot of charisma, and if he develops, he has a chance to be one of the top draws in basketball."

Still, whenever Jordan played Erving, they were the center of attention. The first round went to Erving when he outdunked Michael 3 to 2 and outscored him 21 points to 14 during Jordan's initial trip to Philadelphia to play the 76ers. Michael came back with a staggering 40-point performance in his next visit to the Spectrum in Philly, and since then he has scored a unanimous decision over the Doc. In their final confrontation in the Spectrum on March 24, 1987, Jordan soared to 56 points and emerged as the reigning jam master of the game in the process.

Jordan feels quite honored to be following in the footsteps of the good Doctor. "He represents a way and an image for kids to follow, and in that way I don't mind following Dr. J.," Michael says. "I don't mind taking the leadership he has provided. I want to be a positive image for kids."

You know, if you check out the local playground, you can see those kids in their Air Jordans, sticking out their tongues and attempting to fly. But it's the bigger kids who like to grab the ball with an outstretched hand and rise up to lay the ball softly in the basket as Dr. J. has done so many times. All of which makes Jordan realize, "Quite honestly, there will never be another Dr. J."

And when Erving decided to retire in 1987, it was Jordan who offered to let the Doc take his place in the starting lineup for the all-star game. But then, it was Isiah Thomas who stepped down to let Jordan share that pedestal with Erving. And rightly so, for as Jordan paid his final homage, he said, "Whenever you thought of the NBA, you thought of Dr. J. He was like the founding father."

With Michael, though, the flights have become more prolific. There have been other players who have mastered the art of jamming, but nobody does it better. His reputation precedes him. When he was drafted and came to the Bulls, Orlando Woolridge was the team's resident jam master. But two weeks into the season, Woolridge was asking Michael for lessons. After one particularly crowd-pleasing dunk at Madison Square Garden, Jordan was preparing to leave the Bulls locker room when he spotted Woolridge and called out, "Class is in session tomorrow. You know what I'm talking about."

It has already been established that Jordan is in a class by himself, but never more so than in the realm of dunking. It is not uncommon to see Michael take off and come back down to Earth having done something that makes an observer realize, "I've never seen that before." There are many times when he himself admits he's never done that before. He has raised the standards of dunking to the point where an ordinary running one-hander or even a two-hand windmill is for just plain folks. Now there are guys like Spud Webb flying in the path of Jordan's footsteps trying to live up to the following tenets Michael has set down for basketball's most exciting art form:

1. *If you can't hang—don't jump.*

When Jordan went airborne, it wasn't ordinary jumping. The big guys in the game jump—sometimes. Kareem jumps on his skyhook; Akeem jumps to block shots. Minimal jumping is all Larry Bird uses to do what he does; Magic sometimes only gets off one foot when he puts up his fadeaway jumper. Jumping up implies coming down, but when Jordan takes to the air, landing is not necessarily a given.

Jumping can be measured in terms of inches, but nothing short of a stopwatch provides concrete data on hanging. When you jump, the resulting dunk is a one-hand yawner. But when you hang, you can move the ball from right hand to left hand to earn the style points that set the true jam masters above the rest in any slam-dunk contest. Jordan will give a defender a ball fake left, then in one big step to the right hit the heights. While he's still going up, the defenders are coming down, and by hanging Jordan can go through or over a double- or triple-team to jam the ball into the bucket. Clearly, the only defense for this ability is to put four players on him and hope he runs out of hang time by the time he reaches the basket.

Former Bull Jawaan Oldham, a 7-foot behemoth of a center, employed such a tactic when he blocked a last-second shot by Jordan to preserve a New York Knicks victory after guards Rory Sparrow and Gerald Wilkins sandwiched Jordan and after Patrick Ewing bumped him. Said Oldham, "If he would've had just one player on him, he would have made the shot. I let expend most of his airtime on the other three people, and I was just the last one. You have to be a lot taller than him to stop him, and then you still need at least half his hang time."

2. *Don't bring no weak "stuff."*

Once Julius Erving took off from just inside the free-throw line, and with his hand way up high threw down a dunk that rattled the rim. And for a time whenever there was a nearby rim rattling, it meant someone had just come up with one of these power dunks. There have been several players who have been so strong-armed going to the hole that they leave the fiberglass backboard shattered. But once Michael assaulted the rim, it wasn't enough to merely leave it rattling. He has set a standard that makes how much you can do before you jam the ball the strength of the dunk. There have been times when Jordan has gone baseline, taken off on one side of the rim, then glided to the other before swooping down with the ball in his outstretched hand.

3. *If your dunk doesn't have a name, it's lame.*

There are those gurus who might credit Darryl Dawkins with the being the first to name his dunks. In the midst of a game when he was with the Philadelphia 76ers, Dawkins jumped up, pulled the ball back behind his head with two hands, and rattled the rim with so much force he trashed the backboard. In describing the moment, Dawkins called this move his "gorilla dunk." While the moniker is flashy, it isn't truly distinguishing, for Dawkins has no other slam he deems worthy of titling.

Jordan, on the other hand, has his dunks catalogued. He could have the names registered with the Library of Congress in Washington, D.C., and he has others he hasn't told us about because they are patent pending. Like their creator, though, some of Jordan's jams stand out above the rest.

When he takes a running start, and launches from the foul line, shaking the ball all the way before throwing it down, that is his "demoralizer dunk." This move has degrees of difficulty measured by how many times he shakes the ball like a pair of dice. If he's in the open court, he'll show the ball to the crowd while shaking it. If he's in the midst of traffic, Jordan holds the ball high above his head and moves it as if to dare defenders to take a swipe at it. If he's going one-on-one, Jordan will shake the ball in his man's face as if to say, "Don't think you can get it if I really don't want you to."

When Michael swoops in from the side, wraps both his arms around the ball, and rests his elbow on the rim before jamming it in, he is attempting his "rock-a-baby." This is a show-time dunk, something Michael uses as a sure crowd-pleaser during warm-ups or as a move to get him through the semifinal round of a slam-dunk contest. Occasionally, he will unveil this dunk in a game, like when his hang time is exceptional on that night and no one has a chance of stopping him.

And then there is the "cradle jam," perhaps Michael's most renowned dunk. Anytime he is in the open court and his eyes light up, Jordan is preparing to clutch the ball between his wrist and forearm. Then he twirls it a couple times, spreads his legs, and in a roundabout motion finishes off the jam. This is the pride of the fleet, something Jordan has been throwing at us since he was in college. Once Michael first threw this one down, he realized the potential for multiple methods of jamming was boundless.

4. *If you can't name your dunk—don't bring no junk.*

Some of Michael's moves aren't worthy of words for the simple reason that he can't describe them. To name a slam, you have to be able to do it more than once, and there have been times when Michael looks at himself on tape and says, "Was that me? I've never seen that before."

Yet it's those times that Jordan seems to put his upmost effort into making unforgettable. "When people see the way I play the game, the creativity I put into my moves, I want them to remember me as the only guy they ever knew who could do that. Maybe the essence is that I know there's gonna be things I do that people probably won't ever be able to do again."

The no-name dunks are the best, because those are the ones that give Michael his style points. He goes up and does things we never thought possible —like manipulating the ball from his right hand to his left and then back again, all the while in the air, before he jams it. Whenever he does it, he does it in style. "My style is similar to Houdini, the magician who always tried to do things that people didn't think he could do," Jordan explains. "When I play, I have a sense of trying to make tough things look easy. You always wanna do something the people haven't seen."

There was a time when Jordan still had some

things to learn about dunking. His rookie appearance in the NBA slam-dunk contest didn't go according to the fans' plans. Michael didn't even advance to the semifinals of the competition until an error in the scoring expanded that round from four to five competitors. He used a double-pump, one-handed reverse and a double-pump backwards slam to move into the finals against Dominique Wilkins. In the finals, Wilkins outscored Jordan on all three attempts, but Michael figured his time would come. "This being my first time, I didn't know how to prepare my dunks and what the judges were looking for," he said.

Although Jordan was second, he still finished three places ahead of Julius Erving, which meant his rise to the top was beginning. Then, on February 7, 1987, in Seattle, Jordan came up with a flight to remember. With his full-court dash to the most exhilarating demoralizer dunk ever, Jordan soared into the finals of the slam-dunk contest. His opponent was Jerome Kersey of the Portland Trailblazers, but the only obstacle remaining was the heights of the Kingdome. He started the final round by flaunting his hang time in the process of a slashing slam in which he ducked the rim as he floated by. Next came a swooping cradle jam in which he double-pumped the ball underhanded and spread his legs like a parachute to maintain his altitude. With his finale, Jordan began his assault on the hoop from the left side and threw it down with a sideswiping rock-a-baby.

When Jordan was asked how he planned his dunks this time around, he answered, "I never know until I get up there what's going to happen."

He wasn't talking trash, either. Jordan never brings any junk when he goes to dunk, for he has no such thing as a weak stuff. Winning the slam-dunk contest was the crowning achievement, the accomplishment that made Erving willingly move over and grant Jordan rights to all the space above the rim. Now, Michael was on top of the game.

13.

The Rise to the Top

EARLY IN AUGUST 1986, MICHAEL JORDAN began the countdown. All summer he stayed away from basketball for the first time in his life, and all summer he thought about nothing but basketball. Little did Michael realize at the time, however, that as soon as he reported to training camp for the upcoming season his days would be numbered. And at the time, little did anyone else realize that it would take some new math to fully comprehend what Jordan was about to accomplish.

As soon as the exhibition season started, his numbers started coming up: 61, 59, 56, 51, 49, 46, 45, 43, 40. No, Jordan wasn't playing the lottery, but he would eventually turn this 1986–87 season into one long numbers game. In the past, the Bulls were able to count on Michael Jordan, but never to this extent. During this season, Jordan proved he is the most prolific scorer in the game today. In the NBA, the 20-point barrier is the mark the better players shoot for; 30 points is the mark of an outstanding night; and 40 points is in the realm of Bird, Dominique, and perhaps Alex English on his best night. In 85 games including the play-offs, Michael scored 30 or more—usually more—26 times, and he topped the 40-point plateau 28 times. He had 6 games of 50 or more points and was the first player in a long time to top 60. By the way, he did that twice.

Even as the 1987–88 season was set to begin, there were people still calling his numbers of the previous year. He had the top three scoring efforts in the league: 7 of the top 10, 11 of the top 15, and 13 of the top 20. He had 19 games of scoring in the 20's, and he had just 4 games under 20. He never scored less than double figures. When opponents tried to assign a number to keep Jordan under, they talked of "holding" him to 30 points. He finished the season with 3,041 total points, the third highest ever in the history of the league. Jordan joined Wilt Chamberlain as the only player ever to score more than 3,000 points in a single season, and his 37.1 points-per-game average was fifth-best in history. He also led the Bulls in steals and blocked shots, was second in assists, and third in rebounds, and he was one of only three players in the league to top 100 in each of those categories.

When the counting was finally done, even Jordan reckoned that, "This is probably the greatest offensive season I'll ever have." Jordan had counted on such success, or so it seemed, as he was getting motivated for the season. "I've never come into a season more mentally ready to play," he said as he checked into the Deerfield Multiplex practice facility for training camp. "I can't believe it. When I go to sleep at night and when I wake up in the morning, all I think about is basketball. I'm ready. I know I'm going to have a good year." Accordingly, the most logical way to look at this phenomenal season is to paint a picture by the numbers.

When Jordan weighed in during his preseason physical, he added another dimension to the numerous statistics that portray the most accurate picture of his ability. Doctors discovered not only that his foot had completely healed, but that his hang time would not be severely inhibited by all of his 3.29 percent body fat. As one guru noted in amazement, that is the same amount of body fat the average person sitting behind the average desk possesses in his left earlobe.

Perhaps the Bulls front office knew what it was doing for a change when it changed the team advertising slogan from "A Whole New Breed" to "Rolling Thunder," for the head honchos hoped Jordan would roll into the season with a flurry. In an exhibition-season—opening loss to the Lakers October 10, Michael started the ball rolling with 44 points on 14-of-20 shooting from the field and 16-of-18 from the foul line. In 10 minutes of playing against triple-teaming two nights later against Portland he scored 20 points, and then he led the Bulls to a 97–85 win over Utah with 39 points+ to help garner the first victory for Doug Collins, the third head coach Jordan was playing for in as many years as a pro.

Jordan continued to make his points when the Bulls rolled into Chapel Hill, North Carolina, to play their annual game in the place Michael calls home. This game, however, was on homecoming weekend and it was the debut of the "Dean Dome," the new basketball facility at Carolina named after the venerable Tar Heel mentor. But no one ever counted on the type of numbers Jordan would account for in this game. Not only did he score 36 points and exhilarate the crowd with some resounding dunks, but in two days Carolinians purchased 22,500 tickets for the game, a few thousand more than the number of fanatics who crowd into the Chicago Stadium once in a while. Jordan added a 31-point effort in a 111–103 win over Indiana in his last outing of the preseason, and for those 8 games he averaged 33 points and 33 minutes per contest.

But even the gurus of the game would never have figured on the numbers Jordan would roll up once the regular season tipped off. Eventually, the pencil-pushing statisticians of the NBA would have to resort to keeping a running tally of Jordan's output because they couldn't keep up with his numbers any other way.

So when Michael stepped on to the court at Madison Square Garden in New York for the season opener it was if he was calling his own number. He walked by Collins, looked him in the eye, and told him, "Coach, I'm not going to let you lose your first game." Then, in leading the Bulls to a 108–103 victory over the Knicks, Jordan ran off 50 points to set a record for most points ever scored by an opposing player in the Garden. And after spending the first half dominating the game with steals, assists, and blocked shots, Michael showed the Bulls could count on him most in the stretch run when he scored 21 points in the fourth quarter to make good on his promise to the coach. He was so magnificent, Michael turned a broken play into an alley-oop slam, and with 22 seconds left and the

Bulls ahead 102–100 he took three Knicks to the hoop and hit a soft bank shot in the midst of such traffic.

By the second game of the season, Michael confirmed that when the chips were down, he would put up the numbers. The Bulls traveled to Cleveland November 2, and with 1:41 to play, Michael and his mates were facing a 1-point deficit. Jordan then scored the last 8 points of the game, including the final 2 on free throws after he had been knocked to the ground while going for a game-ending slam. As Jordan rose from his crash to floor, Collins asked him if he would be able to shoot his free throws. Michael merely replied, "You better never take me out." Two games into the season, and there was no counting out Michael Jordan.

As the Bulls rolled to their third straight victory, a 111–104 triumph over San Antonio, Chicago fans were getting in the habit of counting down the time until Jordan would light up the game. With the Bulls trailing 86–75 after three quarters, Michael turned it on to score 16 of his 34 points in the final 12 minutes. His basket, with 3:58 to play, put the team ahead for good. Two nights later, Jordan scored 33 points against Detroit but in the end even he was outnumbered and a last-second, second-effort to pull out the victory came up short.

The next night, November 8, Michael scored 39 points and brought down the curtain on a 101–96 victory over Phoenix with a breakaway cradle jam. In the end, Phoenix coach John MacLeod figured out what all the other coaches were talking about. "Jordan is so great, it takes five guys just to hold him to 20 points." Already, in the first week of the season Jordan wasn't holding back. He was averaging 39.4 points per game, 5.6 rebounds, 2.8 steals —numbers good enough to make him the NBA player of the week in the initial week of the season. And that was only a fraction of what Michael was going to produce.

For all the points Jordan scored, it seemed each basket was more spectacular than the last. In a 112–110 victory over Atlanta November 12, Michael scored the game-winning hoop on a hang-time hot shot with three defenders hanging all over him. Said Collins, "It was your routine, twisting, 360-degree, double-pump, reverse lay-up."

It was all becoming part of a routine for Jordan. With the Bulls sporting a 5–2 record, Boston came to town on November 14. Jordan and Larry Bird turned the first half into a glorified one-on-one with Michael striking for 21 points and Bird coming back with 28. In the second half, Jordan keyed a 10-point Chicago run with 3 hoops to bring the Bulls within 8 points at 73–65. Bird scored 4 straight, but Michael came with 6 of his own to make it 77–73. Michael hit a soft jumper to make it 84–83 with 9:48 left, but the Bulls never managed to take the lead. Jordan converted a 3-point play to make it 94–92 and eventually finished the 48 points to Bird's 37, and it just didn't figure that the Bulls could lose a game in which Jordan had been so brilliant.

There was no figuring Michael this season. When it seemed like he had pushed his prowess to the limit, he set down a new measure for his greatness. In a November 21, come-from-desperation victory over the Knicks at the Stadium, Jordan set an NBA record by scoring the Bulls' final 18 points in a

101–99 win. In the last 6 minutes and 29 seconds, Jordid did what no men had ever done before: he scored from inside and outside, against one defender, two defenders, and three defenders. With the scored tied at 97 with 13 seconds left, Jordan took three dumbfounded Knicks to the hole and hit a running bank shot. New York's Gerald Wilkins popped a 20 footer with 8 seconds left, and Michael then took the ball on a drive to history. As he went past the bench, Collins screamed, "Take it to the hole." Michael hit a stunning 22-foot shot, the fallout of which rocked the Stadium. Even Collins was left considerably dazed by Jordan's performance, which included 3 steals during the final 2 minutes and 40 points in total. "Somehow, every single game has come down to the last few minutes," the coach commented, "and it's kind of nice to have a nuclear weapon on your team."

The Bulls were 7–3 and ready to begin a trip to the West Coast in which Jordan would leave everyone from Jack Nicholson to Magic Johnson shaking their heads. He scored 37 points in a last-second loss at Denver, but he finished the first four weeks of the season with a 37.4 average, a number that made him the NBA's player of the month. And in the next nine games he would run off a streak of mathematical proportions. Those responsible for keeping track of Jordan's points during the next two weeks would need more than an adding machine.

For those of you scoring at home, get your pencils and your scorecards ready: in front of a star-studded crowd, which included Emilio Estavez and Rob Lowe, Jordan took an NBA record 43 shots, hitting on 19 en route to 41 points in a loss to the Los Angeles Lakers. It was the most points scored against the Lakers during their championship season and it tied a Forum scoring record set by Jerry West in 1969. In the next game against Seattle, Jordan really started to generate some talk.

Michael soared by SuperSonics Xavier McDaniel to an apparent basket with 46 seconds left in the Bulls overtime victory, so the Seattle forward began talking trash at Jordan and poked him in the face. Jordan said, "In your face," in the form of 2 free throws, a block of a shot by 6-foot-9 Tom Chambers, then popped a 17-foot jumper right in McDaniel's face to seal the 115–109 triumph. His 40 points marked the seventh time in 14 games he had hit that figure. The next night, December 3, the sum total of Jordan's efforts was 45 points— including 6 straight points to give the team an 86–85 lead with 3:59 to play and a towering dunk over 7-foot-4 Mark "Mount" Eaton—in a 99–94 loss at Utah. His fifth-straight 40-point game—43, to be exact—came in a loss to Phoenix, and the only lining in the dark cloud over a loss at San Antonio on December 6 was Jordan's 40 points as the streak reached six.

When the Bulls returned home on December 8, Jordan greeted the fans with a 40-point effort that featured 8 of the team's final 12, the last hoop on a twisting lay-up, in a 106–100 win over Denver. When Jordan scored 41 in a loss at Atlanta, it was the eighth straight game of 40 or more.

Now there was considerable talk of Jordan having a shot at the record of 14 straight 40-plus games Wilt Chamberlain rolled up in 1961 or the streak of 10 Wilt compiled in 1962. Chamberlain is simply the greatest scorer ever in the history of the game; once he scored 100 points in a single contest and averaged 50.4 points per game for an entire season. But if Jordan needed to provide any legitimacy to be grouped in such company, he did so December 12 by jumping center to start a game at Milwaukee. As the streak hit nine games, Michael scored 41 points to lead the Bulls to a 106–93 victory, their first win at the Mecca since December 22, 1983.

Considering Chamberlain had almost 7 inches on Jordan, his streak was of even greater proportions. And if Jordan was indeed immortal, then no man could bring the streak to an end. And so it was that the roll finally ceased in a game against Milwaukee only because Jordan crash-landed after a drive to the hoop with 5 seconds left in the first half and played for but a few moments in the second half after lying on the court for almost 6 minutes without moving as a result of his great fall. Fortunately, it was just the streak and not the season that ended for Michael.

The thing about Jordan, though, is that he never takes an injury lying down. In fact, he is the type of player who can be knocked down and come back standing taller and stronger than ever. After taking that fall against Milwaukee, he came back to score 41 points in a win over New Jersey on December 16. The strained hamstring and twisted ankle he suffered in the process only seemed to fuel his desire. After a day of rest, Michael struck for 40 points in a win at Indiana, which marked the eleventh time in the last 12 games that he hit the 40's. The latest performance was so impressive that Bobby Knight stopped by to pay his respects to

Jordan afterward. "Bobby said he was the one who taught you how to jump so high," one reporter relayed to Jordan. "Yeah, he did," Michael responded. "He yelled, and I jumped."

When everyone stood around expecting Jordan to take control in the fourth quarter of a game against Utah in which Michael was "held" to 27 points, Jazz coach Frank Layden was a little more complimentary than Knight. "Michael Jordan mesmerizes me. I forget about the game and think I'm at burlesque. He takes me right out of the game. I forget I'm coaching." After he scored 43 points in a 108–92 win over Cleveland December 23, the entire nation wanted to watch Jordan.

And December 25 the nation awoke to find Michael Jordan on its living room televisions, right next to the tree. The Bulls were making their first non-play-off national television appearance with Jordan, and the executives at CBS were calling this game against the Knicks in Madison Square Garden on Christmas Day "a Michael Jordan showcase." Apparently, now Jordan was also good for ratings points. "He is definitely an individual whose super talent, style, and personality make him a draw on television," said Susan Kerr, a spokesperson for CBS. "Most people will watch this game because of Michael Jordan." By his own reckoning, Michael realized, "Ratings are going to be up. We'll be like the 'Bill Cosby Show.'" But the Knicks had a present for Jordan: two players joined Gerald Wilkins in shadowing Michael wherever he went. Even the television cameras couldn't get a clear shot because of the blanket coverage, and it was not a merry day for Michael. He scored 30 points on 10-of-28 shooting and the Bulls lost the game 86–85 when Patrick Ewing hit a shot just before the final buzzer.

Any loss makes Jordan sick, but this one left him with a particular ill will. Two nights later, Michael came to play with a 101-degree fever and the flu, yet he still scored 44 points in leading the Bulls to a 105–93 victory. He hit 20 of 29 shots from the field and turned in such an immaculate performance that no one ever suspected the numbers on the thermometer were up so high. "When I'm sick, I always play better," Jordan said. "My concentration level is much higher. You know, you have to fight off sickness." He was so tough that he managed to score the team's final 10 points in the last 53 seconds of a loss to Golden State despite a chest cold.

If Jordan wasn't running on empty at this point, was he running out of points? Could he possibly continue to produce at this rate? What more could the Bulls ask him to do? Well, with the start of the new year, Collins asked Jordan to move from his big guard position to small forward so the coach could use Jordan on the floor at the same time with newfound scoring threats John Paxson and Sedale Threatt in the backcourt. And like so many times during this season, all Collins had to do was ask, and he shall receive. In his first effort at the new position, Michael scored 34 points in a loss at Boston.

There were those who said Jordan couldn't maintain his vicious scoring pace, especially from his new position. Philadelphia's Charles Barkley said he would break Jordan before letting him score more than 40 points. "You can bet on it," the Round Mound of Rebound issued as a warning to

Jordan. Under such circumstances, Jordan is a betting man, and if there's one thing he likes better than a number's game, it's defying the odds. He was right on the money with 47 points in a 124–118 win over Detroit, including 17 in the fourth quarter.

Two nights later, January 9, against Portland, Jordan came up with another golden moment. With 5:10 left in the fourth quarter, Jordan posted low against Trailblazers Clyde Drexler. As soon as he received the entry pass, Portland's Jim Paxson came over to double team. A quick spin and Jordan blew by Drexler and Paxson, then glided by center Caldwell Jones and Jerome Kersey to kiss an over-the-shoulder, reverse lay-up high off the glass and into the bucket for 2 of his 53 points in the Bulls' 121–117 victory. Even four defenders couldn't hold Michael down in this game as he assumed the small-forward position and hit 20 of 34 shots from the floor to go with 5 assists, 3 steals, and 2 blocked shots.

Jordan was becoming a target, so to speak. A kind of basketball-playing gunslinger who would face "High Noon" every time he stepped onto the court. The next showdown came January 18 at the Stadium when the Philadelphis 76ers came to town with a bread truck named Charles Barkley leading the way. In so many words, Barkley said he had come to hunt down Jordan, promising to "break" him before letting him score 37 points as he had the previous meeting between the two teams. Breaking Jordan, however, is impossible. Barkley may have had a better shot at sitting on him to squash Jordan, or perhaps Boy Gorge might devour Michael whole if he was really hungry.

Jordan, however, ate Barkley alive by scoring 47 points to go with 10 rebounds and 6 assists. He finished off the job by scoring 16 points in the fourth quarter to help lock up a 105–89 victory.

Finally, all the scoring was beginning to take something out of Jordan. After he scored 32 points, including 14 in the fourth quarter in a loss at Indiana, Michael was preoccupied with what other people were thinking. "Expectations are always going to be high if you continue to play well. If I score 40 points, people will want me to score 50. That's just the way society thinks." After scoring 35 points, with an unexpected 20 in the third quarter in a win over Cleveland on January 23, Jordan came back to tally 49 in a loss at Philadelphia, which caused Sixers coach Matt Goukas to speculate on what more Jordan could do. "Can he score every Bulls point in a game? I'd certainly like to see him try. He is certainly capable of doing it."

Forty-two games into the regular season—one more than halfway—Jordan was averaging 37.2 points per game to lead the league in scoring by almost a 10-point margin. The numbers continued to pile up when Jordan received more than 1.4 million votes for the all-star game to break the record for most votes Magic Johnson set the year before. Expectations being what they are, most of those 1.4 million fans wanted nothing more than to see Jordan dominate the all-star game, like he had most every other game so far during the season.

Expectations being what they are, however, it is impossible even for Jordan to fulfill all of them. He struggled through his second all-star game with a mere 11 points on 5 of 12 shooting in 28 minutes. Reasoned Jordan, "I was a little tentative, but that was because I was playing out of position at point guard. My job as point guard was to spread the ball around. I couldn't look for my shots like normal."

The thing about Jordan is that he can make his fans forget one dismal performance by coming up with an unforgettable effort. In his first outing after the all-star game, Jordan overcame a bruised wrist and a black eye to score 45 points in a win over Seattle. He scored 16 points in the final period, including 11 of the Bulls' final 15. "It's been a bumps-and-bruises season for me so far," he said, "but that's not going to keep me from competing." Yes, Michael was back to his old self.

There are some things about Michael during this season that just did not compute, though. He led the league in minutes played, for example, with 3,281, which figures to an average of more than 38 of the 48 per game. In a 124–120 overtime win over Sacramento, Jordan played every minute of the second half and the extra period, and hit 2 free throws with 10 seconds left to tie the game and send it into overtime. He had already scored nine points to key a 13–4 run that tied the game at 112.

For all the double- and triple-teaming, Jordan was overcoming the odds despite being outnumbered. But it wasn't until February 20 that someone figured a way to stop Michael. In the past, opponents tried to deny Jordan the ball, and when he did get it, it was a quick turn and he was airborne toward the basket. But on this night, the opposition let him get the ball and sent a blitz of defenders at him as if he were Walter Payton having just taken a handoff. Such strategy seems difficult to execute, and it was only the soon-to-be world champion Lakers who could pull it off. But with two-time NBA defensive player of the year Michael Cooper leading the rush, Jordan was only "held" to 33 points.

But it was the Lakers, and the Lakers alone, who could pull it off. In the next game, a 113–103 win over Atlanta, Jordan struck for 43 points, 6 assists, 5 blocked shots, and a personal best of 8 steals. Once again, you only had to refer to the numbers to evaluate this performance. He dominated the first three quarters with 39 points, and in the first 6 minutes of the game he had 4 baskets, 3 steals, and 2 assists. During a 5-minute stretch in the third quarter, he scored 15 points and had 3 baskets and a steal in 63 seconds.

The season was no longer merely a numbers game. Jordan was preparing to lead the Bulls to the play-offs and turn the record book into a catalogue of his personal records. On February 27, Michael scored 58 points in a win over New Jersey to break the Bulls' regular-season, single-game scoring record of 56 set by Chet Walker in 1972. He hit 16 of 25 from the field and added 26 of 27 from the foul line, the latter of which was the third-highest free throw total in NBA history. He scored 17 points in each of the first two quarters, and had the Bulls last 11 in the opening period. He added 15 of the final 17 in the second quarter, and when the Nets came within 102–86, Jordan scored 10 of the team's next 16. He made his final point with a soaring-reverse lay-up on which he was fouled. He added the final free throw, and with 2:44 left he exited to a capacity crowd cheering in anticipation of the day Jordan would top this mark.

That night came just a week later when Jordan left the fans at the Pontiac Silverdome roaring for more after scoring 61 points in a 125–120 overtime win for the Bulls. This was a fourth quarter to remember. He scored 26 points in the period—the most ever in one quarter against the Pistons—including the team's first 13, 24 of the first 26, and 26 of the 33 in total. In the final seconds, he hit a hanging fall-away jumper to tie the game, and preserved a chance at victory by stealing the ball from Isiah Thomas when Detroit was working for a last shot.

Just when it seemed like he couldn't do any more, he did it again. When he came back to the Spectrum on March 12, the noise from the crowd wanted him to play it again, man, so Michael scored 49 points to tie the stadium record he had set there a little more than a month ago. He returned to the scene of his December scoring streak, and scored 40 points against the Los Angeles Clippers in front of the same witnesses and other stars like Timothy Hutton, Debra Winger, and O.J. Simpson who joined Nicholson. He displayed a variety of acrobatic moves, and on one play he split two defenders on a flight to the basket, missed a reverse lay-up, grabbed the rebound in the midst of three Clippers, and missed that, thereby proving he doesn't have to score to excite the crowd. "All the people came out to see me play, and to see if all the ink about Michael Jordan was true," he said afterward. "I'm pleased, the crowd is pleased, and we won the game."

When you're hot, you're hot. Jordan continued to light it up under the bright lights of the West Coast with a 40-point effort in a win at Sacramento and 46 points in a loss at Portland. On March 25, however, Jordan may have come up with his most timely performance of the year. After Chicagoans paid homage to Julius Erving on his final stop in the Windy City, Jordan provided a tribute of his own by scoring 56 points in a 93–91 victory over the Sixers. Even the good Doctor was amazed by such numbers as he had never put up. Michael was averaging 37.3 points per game and 2.77 steals. He had 107 blocked shots, which was more than 14 starting centers. Such statistics were already enough to support Jordan's being the most valuable player in the league.

He certainly was invaluable to the Bulls and the NBA. He continued to fill every stadium he played in, and without having to follow Jordan, what would the league's statisticians be doing? But finally, Jordan was able to bask in some of the glory of his accomplishments. After scoring 36 points to lead the Bulls to a 101–75 triumph over Washington on March 31, Jordan kicked back on the bench with Charles Oakley as they started joking and poking with one another. The Bulls had just made the play-offs for the third year in a row, and that was the only number Michael cared about.

By the first week of April, Jordan began gearing up to battle in the play-offs. As he was finishing off a fast break in a game against Detroit, Pistons Bill Laimbeer tried to knock Jordan out of midair. Michael scrambled to his feet and went after Laimbeer, later claiming, "I think he did it on purpose." Jordan then proceeded to knock out the Pistons with 39 points in the Bulls' 118–86 superior decision. On April 13, Jordan was so hot in scoring 53 points against Indiana he single-handedly took the edge off one of Chicago's biting April snowstorms. He hit his first 5 shots, and 14 of his first 18. At one point of the fourth quarter he brought the ball up court and either scored a basket or free throws on 7 consecutive possessions for 13 straight points. More numbers for thought: this was the sixth time he had scored more than 50 points and his 35th game over 40 in his NBA career.

The seventh and 36th, respectively, came the next night when Jordan hit for 50 in a win at Milwaukee, With two games remaining in the regular season, Jordan was just 37 points short of 3,000. For the past four games, Michael was averaging 44 points, 7 rebounds, 6.5 assists, and 4 steals per game.

But there was no accounting for what Jordan would do in the next game. Even his scoring 61 points in a 117–114 loss to Atlanta was overshadowed on this April 16 night. He scored his 3,001st point on, of all shots, a follow-up lay-up to join Chamberlain as the only players to reach such a plateau. It was his third consecutive game of 50 or more points; only Chamberlain did that, too. He had 23 consecutive points in the last 6:33 of the first half and the first 2:12 of the second. Wilt never did that. There was a point when the Hawks ran out of ways to stop Jordan, so coach Mike Fratello bowed in front of his bench, and said, "I said a good novena." This was truly a religious experience.

Jordan finished the regular season with 3,041 points, the third highest total ever. Now the case for him as the MVP was complete, for as columnist Bernie Lincicome of the *Chicago Tribune* wrote, "If Michael Jordan is not the player of the year, Moses Malone wears lace undies."

Still, Michael's days of this season were numbered. Jordan scored 35 and 42 points in the first two games of the play-offs against the Celtics, but the Bulls lost both games in Boston. Jordan was convinced the team could take the Celtics when the series returned to Chicago, but that too did not work out as he figured. The Bulls lost the third game, and as Jordan sat in front of his locker afterward, he had no more reason to make a point. He had just finished the greatest offensive season he could ever have, yet the NBA was going for another two months without him. In the end, the feeling his face displayed was ominous. Jordan would have traded all those 3,041 points, all those 40-, 50-, and 60-point games, if, at the end of the season, he could be there saying, "We're number one."

14.

Fan-demonium

MICHAEL JORDAN PREPARED TO PLAY HIS game, but his path to the hole on this afternoon was unexpectedly blocked. For all the hours he spent trying to solve persistent triple-teaming defense, this time he had no answer for the impasse which was fronting him. If only this was Magic or the Bird or Joe Dumars or a triumvirate of New York Knicks in his way—well, then, Michael could jump over them all and drop the ball in the bucket.

Except Michael Jordan was on a golf course now, and the crowd was closing in on him with every second. He went to his left, and then back to his right, but he couldn't satisfy these autograph hounds of all ages. Security guards tried to clear the court—rather the putting green—but this was becoming a sign of the times for Michael.

On a muggy Tuesday afternoon in Oak Brook, Illinois, a small, affluent suburb of Chicago, Jordan joined Walter Payton, Ernie Banks, Mike Ditka and Bill Murray to compete in the Beatrice Western

Open Pro-Celebrity shootout golf tournament. The event was a fund-raiser as part of the famed Western Open Golf Tournament, and on a Tuesday the crowd was much bigger than what would come through the gates that weekend for the real thing. Kids and adults chased Jordan all across the golf course. They used Payton as a pick and headed for Jordan, almost shunning Murray in the process. That's the fact, Jack. After the tournament was over, the crowd followed Jordan into the clubhouse and the locker room until his only escape was the shower. That's the fact, Jack.

Hero worship had never been practiced to such extremes. Suddenly, a crowd of near-hysterical people formed outside a Bigsby & Kruthers' store in a suburban Chicago shopping mall, where Jordan was the center of attention again. In Pittsburgh, where the NBA doesn't even have a team, Jordan was surrounded by fast-breaking fans while making an appearance for Coca-Cola, and only a white stretch limousine provided him a great escape. In San Diego, Jordan was taping a segment of the television show "Greatest Sports Legends," when the only place he could find with enough privacy to change clothes happened to be behind an equipment truck.

The signs of the time of Jordan becoming the single greatest sports superstar in the world were more than Air-apparent. Michael wasn't just a featured guest on "Greatest Sports Legends," he was the host of the show. When he went to throw out the first pitch at a Pittsburgh Pirates' baseball game, even the umpire stopped him to ask for an autograph. He had his own video game; Michael Jordan products took up an entire page of the

Spiegel Catalogue for Christmas 1988. Tourists came to Chicago from Europe and they wanted to see Michael Jordan. He dated Robin Givens before Mike Tyson.

He had signed a contract to make him the highest-paid player in the game, and off the court he was earning almost twice as much as he was on the court. His immortality may have been confirmed when he became the first basketball player to grace the cover of a box of Wheaties for national distribution. His national appeal was the greatest in professional sports, and perhaps even Bob Hope may have been a bit envious of Michael's endorsement opportunities.

As freelance writer David Breskin surmised in a story for the March 1989 issue of *Gentleman's Quarterly* (catch Michael on the cover in a brilliant Glen-plaid wool double-breasted brown suit), "people are not only awed by Michael Jordan, they like him. They believe him. Somehow, he manages to be both the downest brother and the whitest bread at the same time. That Jordan reconciles the opposites within his own character so smoothly has made him the most admired, idolized and moneyed team-sport hero in the entire American-hero business. In fact, for some folks he has come to represent America—as in, we may not make cars or televisions too well, but we turn out a helluva Michael Jordan."

Only five years into his professional career and Michael Jordan had become a popular cult figure, something seen by more than just that sweat band pushed halfway up the left forearm of kids (and adults) on playgrounds across America. Who else has been so well chronicled by attendance figures and income earned? If he wasn't a cult figure, he certainly had a cult following, and the best part of it is that all the clamor didn't even bother Michael. He liked it, and that's a fact, Jack.

"It took some getting used to, but now I enjoy all the off-court stuff. It's like being back in school. I'm learning all the time. In college, I never realized all the opportunities available to a pro athlete. I've been given the chance to meet all kinds of people, to travel and expand my financial capabilities, to get ideas and learn about life, to create a world apart from basketball."

Yet in his world apart from the game, Jordan drew more of a crowd than when he had the basketball. Every time he would show up at Chicago's O'Hare Airport to embark on another road trip, it would be only a matter of moments before he was besieged by the masses with pens in hand. Michael always, always obliged with as many autographs as possible before airport security escorted him into a private room for the safety of everyone involved. "It's like traveling with a rock star," said one teammate. It always will be.

But Michael J. never tried to keep people out of his world. It seems the crowd forever kept coming at him with a lifelong full-court press, and Jordan knew if he smiled they smiled back. Sitting in the chair of his favorite barber shop, Michael could only be amused when the kids pressed their noses against the front window to get a look at him getting a haircut. Or two. He had to sneak out the back door into the alley, but he waited before getting into his Corvette because he knew someone wanted an autograph. Or two.

When he was growing up in Wilmington, Michael had gone to church on Sundays. He continued the practice while he was at North Carolina. He still takes time to pray when he's alone, but four years into his pro career Michael Jordan could no longer go to church without being made to feel like the Savior. "When I go to church, any church, everybody stares. I went back to my own church in Wilmington a few times since I've been in the pros, and it really hasn't been the same. It's more or less, 'Well, Michael is here today; let's have him speak for us.'"

Jordan became so popular he was immortalized in ways sports publicists never imagined. He became a regular character in the comic strip "Shoe," and he wasn't enshrined only in print. Don Transeth makes computer games for Electronic Arts, the company which produced the video computer game "Julius Erving goes one-on-one with Larry Bird." After Erving retired in 1987, Transeth came to Chicago to talk to Michael for input into his new game, "Larry Bird goes one-on-one with Michael Jordan." Said Transeth: "It seemed like the logical thing to do."

If Michael Jordan were only a great basketball player, would he be so popular? Larry Bird had won three times the amount of Most Valuable Player awards as Michael coming into the 1988–89 season, and Bird could rarely be seen off the court, except for a beef commercial. Magic Johnson was articulate, and full of charisma, as well. But Michael was the fans' favorite—the top vote-getter for the NBA All-Star Game in both 1988 and 1989—because he was sincere, which may have been his greatest star quality of all. One Halloween he wasn't going to be home, so he left a note on his door asking trick-or-treaters to come back. He gave them all free Big Macs when they did.

"In the age of TV sports, if you were to create a media athlete and star for the '90's—spectacular talent, mid-sized, well-spoken, attractive, accessible, old-time values, wholesome, clean, natural, not too Goody Two-shoes, with a little bit of deviltry in him—you'd invent Michael," says David Falk, Jordan's agent. "He's the first modern crossover in team sports. We think he transcends race, transcends basketball. In other words, he's up there with Spuds MacKenzie."

When it comes to commercial appeal, even Spuds seems to be a distant second to Michael. We already know about all the different business deals Jordan is into. At the beginning of 1989, he added Wheaties to the Jordan line, which already included Coke, McDonald's, Chevrolet, Nike, Johnson products, Wilson and Guy Larouche watches. As he rose to the top in 1988 and 1989, the Michael Jordan in-your-home, free-standing mini-basketball game enveloped the toy market.

Jordan sells because of his marketability. He really does eat Chicken McNuggets right out of the bag, and he loves to wear his Air Jordans right out of the box. "Sometimes I change them every three or four hours," he says. In the midst of the NBA Game of the Week, you might see Jordan leaning on the hood of a Chevy Blazer, telling the true story behind the legend of his tongue—and you feel like driving a Chevy.

Sometimes it's easy to underestimate Jordan's net worth in the corporate realm. Nike very nearly made such a mistake in November 1988. The original contract Michael signed with the shoe company was about to expire, when Pro-Serv suggested that Jordan was deserving of the richest shoe endorsement contract ever and more than twice the original deal. Nike said no deal, and added that the "Air" logo initially had nothing to do with Jordan. All this after "Air Jordan" shoes and products grossed more than $100 million in its first year.

But on Feb. 17, 1989—Michael's 26th birthday —Nike came forward with an offer for reportedly at least $20 million over seven years. Nike sources said the deal was believed to be the richest shoe-endorsement contract ever. The new deal also accorded Jordan input and veto powers in the design of the shoe. A press conference was arranged to close the deal and televised live via satellite. Nike made an even more momentuous occasion by serving up a three-foot-high, 50-pound birthday cake to Michael in the form of an Air Jordan shoe.

Nike commissioned film director Spike Lee to make another series of commercials for the Jordan line. Lee donned the persona of ultra-nerd Mars Blackman, who in one spot loses his superfine girlfriend Nola Darling to Michael because he is garbed in the newest Air Jordans. "I never said they were strictly for basketball," Jordan muses. Mars finishes off the session by standing over the basket and reminding us, "You cannot do this," but is he talking about a high-flying, death-defying 360-slam dunk, or the way Michael captivates audiences?

Wherever he went, Jordan never failed to pack the place on or off the court. As far as court royalties were concerned, the Bulls figured to gross

$10 million in ticket revenue alone during fiscal year 1988. In Jordan's fourth season as a pro, the Bulls set an all-time attendance record—which held up for exactly one year. That was 1989 when the average crowd for a basketball game in Chicago was 18,042. In 1984, the Bulls were drawing an average of 6,365 per night. In 1986–87, the Bulls sold out 14 of 41 home games; in 1987–88, all but one game was a sellout. That one game was the last in the Jordan era to not be a sellout.

Two days after the Bulls set the attendance record in 1988, the franchise decided it was time to share some of the return on investment. During that season, Jordan stood to earn about $880,000 in salary, including incentives. But Bulls owner Jerry Reinsdorf offered Jordan a raise. Beginning in fiscal year 1989, Jordan signed an eight-year deal worth $25 million, which made him the highest-paid player in the NBA. The league's gurus and its greatest players received the news of the deal and responded in unison, "Deservedly so."

So how many times can you be a multi-millionaire? With the new endorsements and new contract, Jordan merely had to expand the staff which handles his business affairs to eight. Deloris and James became vice presidents of JUMP, and Larry stepped in to run Flight 23, the sporting goods stores Jordan opened in North Carolina. Michael, in the meantime, took care of the advertising. The last time you saw him wearing something without a Nike logo was when he was sporting one of his Bigsby & Kruthers suits.

But it's not the money which has cultivated this mystique about Michael. "Ordinary people see the good things: the money, the fame, the celebrity status. You've got to have a personality that fits the mold. If I was an introverted person, it would be tough to be in a situation like this.

"But I'm such an extroverted person. I'm outgoing and I like being around people. I don't try to isolate myself from the public. If I run into people who ask for my autograph, I'm able to deal with that without a problem. But if it wasn't for my basic personality, which comes from my parents, there's no way I could deal with the position I'm in."

For proof of Michael's way with people, consider the following situation: Richie Weaver is a home boy high school hoopster from Atlanta who has taken Jordan-worshipping to the limit. According to informed sources, Weaver has seven posters of Michael on his bedroom wall, six pairs of Air Jordans and five golden homemade highlight films on videotape. On Feb. 17, 1988, Weaver brought a cake to school and threw a 25th birthday party for Jordan.

On a sunny summer afternoon, Weaver traveled to Kenny Rogers' ranch in Georgia to watch Michael compete with Isiah Thomas, Dominique Wilkins, Larry Bird and others in a celebrity sportsstar tournament. The last event of the competition was bass fishing, which is something Jordan has never done. He can't even swim. But Michael went out there in a boat and beat Isiah, Dominique and the Bird, and caught more fish than the rest of them combined. Weaver showed his support, and though it was against the rules of the outing, Jordan autographed a pair of Weaver's shoes. He spent an entire day waiting for the autograph, and now Richie can go home a wealthy man.

"As far as being on a pedestal, it's a compliment,

yet it's somewhat painful to me that one person can be viewed so high above other people," Michael said. "For example, if I go to a restaurant, I am likely to get that meal free. But poor people who go to the same restaurant have got to wash dishes to eat. And I'm the one who can afford it. If you can explain that, then you can explain society and you can explain Richie Weaver looking up to me."

Explain, however, how members of the San Francisco Giants baseball team could answer the question "If you could pick one athlete to try out for the Giants, who would it be," in the fashion they did.

Manager Roger Craig: Michael Jordan. "I'd put him in center field, and he could jump into the second deck to catch home runs. He'd be like Willie Mays—a guy who could do everything."

Catcher Bob Brenly: "I'd have to go with Michael Jordan. No matter what he did, he'd have to be able to help."

Vice President of baseball operations Bob Kennedy: "Michael Jordan; I'd play him anywhere he wanted."

Pitching coach Norm Sherry: "I don't know any of their names. Who's that guy in Chicago who flies through the air? Him."

So if Michael Jordan hasn't become the world's greatest sports cult figure, then why is it Lt. Col. Douglas Kirkpatrick of the U.S. Department of Astronautics even has something definitive to say about the man? Can you think of another superstar who conjures up the following description: "Michael Jordan has overcome the acceleration of gravity by the application of his muscle power in the vertical plane, thus producing a low-altitude earth orbit."

So what, then, is the price of fame? Well, Michael can't go to the movies, walk down the street or go shopping in a mall without drawing a crowd. "I'd like to go out for dinner without having to ask for a table in the corner," he says. At 26 years old, Michael Jordan can't even hang out on a public playground and just shoot some hoops with the home boys. Remember this is a guy who autograph seekers wouldn't hesitate to follow into the shower for a moment of his time.

That's the fact, Jack.

15.

Super Human

THE MAN IN THE BURNT ORANGE POLO shirt four rows behind the basket beamed an expression that belied description. Yet such a look was the best—the only—way to convey another magical moment courtesy of marvelous Michael. It was the fifth and final game of the Chicago Bulls' 1989 opening-round playoff series with Cleveland, and in the fourth row of the Richfield Coliseum a very ordinary polo fan stood out in the crowd with his eyebrows raised to excruciating heights and his mouth hanging open wide enough to engulf the basketball in Jordan's hand. Sometimes reactions just speak louder than words.

Jordan at the moment was in mid-flight and in the midst of drilling a game-winning, rim-rattling 18-foot ultra-hang-time jump shot with no time left in the game. For the Bulls, the shot meant one of the greatest playoff upsets in the history of the game. For the man in the orange Polo shirt, well, even in the agony of defeat this was his chance for some national exposure.

The photograph which appeared in newspapers and magazines across the country in the days following Jordan's heroics focused in on Michael in mid-flight. The man in the orange shirt with the look on his face provided the consummate backdrop. "Unfathomable, simply unfathomable," said Cleveland center Brad Daugherty in his best attempt to describe what happened. Cavalier forward Larry Nance merely said, "Michael Jordan . . . superstar," and he left it at that.

As Michael Jordan ascended to his status as the greatest player in the game (check it out, the March 1989 issue of *Gentleman's Quarterly* quoted Magic Johnson as saying, "Everyone talks about how it's me and Larry [Bird]. Really, there's Michael, and then there's everybody else") reactions began to speak louder than mere words of praise. It was as if Michael was playing his own little game of one-on-one with the populace. **Now I'm going to drive the baseline, glide under the basket, turn my back to the defense and kiss a shot in off the glass. Catch me if you can.** Maybe he did it for effect, just to see the look on everyone's face.

During the course of the 1987–88 and 1988–89 seasons, however, Michael Jordan went about leaving everyone in his flight path speechless. Against Phoenix on Jan. 23, 1988, Jordan found himself in mid-flight, back to the basket and no view of the hoop. He whirled in the air and threw in a blind jump shot. Three months later against the Knicks in New York, Jordan jumped up and dunked with Mark Jackson hanging on to his jersey—going along for the ride, you might say. Then there was the time he hit the off-balance, falling, sprawling 24-foot jump shot against Detroit in November of 1987 at the final buzzer to force overtime. And how many times in the 1989 playoffs did he go right at New York's Patrick Ewing or Detroit's Bill Laimbeer on the drive, spin to draw the foul and softly drop in a baby hook shot?

"I was just amazed by his play," said teammate Horace Grant. "Sometimes it's really hard to believe without me being there and witnessing it for myself." These were no mere words of praise. After the shot against Phoenix, backcourtmate Rory Sparrow exclaimed, "When he hit that one shot floating away from the basket, I just jumped up and gave him a standing ovation." When New York Knicks' coach Rick Pitino witnessed Jordan dunk over Jackson in the process of scoring 47 points, he said, "Michael Jordan was as great as I've ever seen him. You just can't stop Jordan. He was like Superman, and I didn't have any Kryptonite."

Before a game against Seattle in Chicago March 11, 1989, yet another sportswriter—this one from a Spanish newspaper—was taking his best shot at describing the essence of Michael Jordan.

"So tell me, Mr. Jordan, what do you need to make your team better?"

Jordan let the tip of his tongue slip out of his mouth as he fought back a grin, then answered, "A cape."

Giving Michael a cape would only have made life more of a mismatch than it already had become. During his fourth and fifth professional seasons (1987–88 and 1988–89), Jordan left all opponents with their mouths hanging open in either amazement or exhaustion. After both seasons, the players themselves named Michael as the league's most valuable player through the annual poll *The Sporting News* publishes. The sportswriters and sportscasters who officially name the NBA's Most Valuable Player gave him the honor in 1988 and made him runner-up to Magic Johnson for a second time in 1989. In the process, he led the Bulls to a 50-win season, a first-round playoff win over the Cavaliers in 1988, and to the NBA Eastern Conference Finals in 1989. Both seasons ended with losses to the Pistons, who had to eventually stick three of their bad, bad boys at a time on Michael to shut him down. Nevertheless, as that 1989 series ended with Detroit, the Pistons' John Salley exclaimed, "I love Magic to death, but after playing against Michael, he is the MVP. It's a shame he didn't get it."

As he won his second and third consecutive scoring titles, was named the NBA's defensive player of the year in 1988 and logged more playing minutes than anyone else in the league, Jordan proved he was more than a man of steel. He was a man of iron, who played with nagging groin injuries, the flu, bad colds and usually played better than most guys did healthy. Was he Superman? Maybe not. Super*human*—most definitely. If he had been Sampson, they might have cut off his hair, except that Michael already had it shaved down to a razor stubble.

It was more than a blind bank shot here, or a whirling dunk there. Other players came up with great shots, but Jordan had entire games of great shots. Once more, when it came to crunch time and the game was on the line, Jordan would come up with memorable moments in abundance. In the fourth quarter, everyone knew he would get the ball, and he would still run off 20 in a row. Against Cleveland on that playoff Sunday of 1989, everyone in the country watching on CBS television knew he was going to get the ball, and he still got it and made the shot.

"Michael Jordan is—well, words cannot explain Michael Jordan," said Charles Davis, a member of the 1988–89 Bulls. "If you have a thesaurus, a dictionary, if you look in Latin or some other language and find a word to do it, let me know. I'm just glad I'm on his side of the fence."

There are not enough words to describe all of Michael's magical moments at this point of his career. There are some, though, that do merit a closer look.

The single greatest tear Michael ever wrought—aside from his 63-point onslaught against the Celtics in the '86 playoffs—unquestionably came against the Pistons April 14, 1988 in front of a CBS television audience. On Easter Sunday in front of 23,712 fans at the Pontiac Silverdome Jordan hit 20 of his first 24 shots on his way to a regular-season 1987–88 NBA-high 59 points. He scored 10 points in a 20–10 Chicago run with 8:33 to play that turned an 80–73 deficit into a 112–100 victory. With 10 seconds left and the game tied at 110, Jordan blocked a shot by Isiah Thomas. He recovered the loose ball and was fouled, then made two free throws with four seconds left. "He was in his own little funk and there was no way I could get him out of it," said Detroit guard Vinnie Johnson. "He hit a few shots that I know even he had to be impressed with himself. There was this one drive to the hole, and three of our guys jumped at him. We swiped at him, spun him around, fouled him, and it still fell in. He felt like he could do anything out there—which is what he did."

At home against Milwaukee Feb. 17, 1989 was one for the books. As Bulls' radio play-by-play man Jim Durham would exclaim every time Michael went up with a shot, "Jordan 20-footer; book it." Michael scored 27 points in the fourth quarter to break the Chicago Stadium record for fourth-quarter points Wilt Chamberlain and Pete Maravich shared with 24. He scored 39 of his 50 points in the second half to tie Chamberlain's record for most points in a half. The 50-point game was the 17th in his career, which tied him with Elgin Baylor for second on the all-time list behind Chamberlain. Oh, and he also hit a 16-foot jumper with one second left to give the Bulls a 117–116 victory. This, by the way, all happened poetically, but perhaps not ironically, on Michael's 26th birthday.

On Feb. 3, 1988, Jordan ran off with one fourth-quarter flurry that provided a case study of how he has turned this into a science: In the fourth quarter, the Bulls were trailing the Lakers 83–67. Twice Jordan drove around Byron Scott, Michael Cooper and Magic Johnson for dunks. Then he floated into the lane for a jumper over James Worthy. Then another. He took Scott one-on-one and went up for the jumper. So did Scott. They hung. Michael hung longer, then swished the soft J. Finally, Michael took off on the break, streaked by Scott and soared over Kareem for a cradle jam. The

Bulls closed to 101–97 before losing 110–101. Michael scored 22 of his 39 in the fourth quarter, and Bulls' assistant coach John Bach may have found the only way to describe the action: "When Michael took over in the fourth quarter, it was like a shark in a feeding frenzy. He sensed the blood in the water and went for it."

Boston's Kevin McHale knew the feeling. Jordan's biggest numbers have come against the Celtics, and he admits "Against teams like the Celtics or the Lakers I have to raise my game to another level." The evening of March 19 was another case in point. Jordan scored 50 points as the Bulls beat Boston 113–103 for their first home victory over the Celtics since Dec. 17, 1985, when Michael scored 46. He scored 17 points in the fourth quarter, and 15 in a 20–10 run that turned a 86–79 lead into a 106–89 runaway. "Jordan single-handedly dismembered and dismantled all of us," McHale said.

Such superheroics had the Bulls up and coming, and the Metropolis of Chicago adored its new savior. Look, up at the top of the NBA standings, there are the Bulls with the best record in the league to start the 1987–88 season. They're 12–3 overall and a remarkable 8–1 on the road. Call the *Daily Planet* and tell them to hold the presses. Isn't this just super?

When Jordan came to training camp, though, the season seemed like it would be anything but super. At practice Oct. 27, Jordan vehemently stormed out 20 minutes before the session was scheduled to end. Seems the Bulls were in the midst of an intrasquad scrimmage when they encountered a scoring discrepancy. Coach Doug Collins said the score was 4–3 with Jordan's team down. Michael begged to differ.

"I know the score was 4–4. I always keep score in everything—scrimmages, games, whatever. I'm a competitor and I want to win. People may think this is trivial. But when you're a competitor and want to win, nothing is trivial."

It wasn't just talk. During Michael's rookie season, then–Bulls coach Kevin Loughery made Jordan switch teams in an intrasquad game when his side was up 7–2. Michael responded by scoring seven straight times and leading his new team to an 11–8 triumph.

But there was no winner in this latest riff. Collins didn't want to discuss the issue publicly, and he said he would wait for Jordan to approach him to solve the problem. After a few days Michael chilled out and went to talk to Collins. "Everything's cool," he announced, and Jordan finished the 1987 preseason with his two best games of the year so far, including 36 points and eight assists in a 124–111 win over Dallas in Chapel Hill, N.C. in the finale. Once the reconciliation had been done, Jordan said, "I'm human."

He used the 1987–88 season to prove otherwise. Consequently, the Bulls provided a November to remember. Michael had 36 on 15-of-25 shooting in a 104–94 win over Philadelphia in the season opener. Only a groin injury slowed Jordan early in the season, but he overcame that to score 31 in a 105–96 win at New Jersey which left the club at 3–0. Two weeks into the season Jordan had a league-leading 33.8 scoring average and Chicago had the best record in the NBA. When Michael came up with 31 points, 10 rebounds and four steals in a 107–102 win at Boston, the rest of the league was looking at the Bulls with raised eyebrows.

Jordan was scoring and the Bulls were soaring. He threw down 49 against the Pistons, who needed a last-second three-point shot by Isiah Thomas and overtime to net a 144–132 win which left the Bulls at 7–2. November came to a close with the Bulls leading the NBA's Central Division at 10–3, the team's best first month of the season since 1973. Jordan was the unanimous choice as the Player of the Month; he was well on his way to being Player of the Year.

Certainly everyone wanted to see Jordan's aerial aerobatics, but what he was doing defensively this season was worth more than a passing glance. Jordan had taken the concept of freelancing defensively which he had learned at North Carolina and made it his own little secret weapon in the NBA. He would float through the passing lanes with the greatest of ease, tip the ball and then scoop it up and soar in for a raid on the rim.

His favorite move defensively would come from the weak side where he could sneak up on the man with the ball in the low post and block a shot from behind. Here was Jordan, all of 6-foot-6, taking on Houston's twin towers, Akeem Olajuwon and Ralph Sampson, and skying. He blocked Akeem, then Ralph, then forced Akeem into a pair of airballs. Call it an Air Jordan sneak attack. In the 112–103 Chicago victory over the Rockets on Dec. 13, Jordan's 44 points and nine assists weren't nearly as important as his five steals and five blocked shots.

"They don't know where I'm coming from, and that's my advantage," Jordan explained. "It's like David sneaking up on Goliath."

Jordan went on to record more than 200 steals and 100 blocked shots for the second straight season. Against the Nets Jan. 30, 1988, he had a team record 10 steals, including six in the third quarter. Michael had made it a point to show off his defense this season. "People see me as just a scorer," he said, "and I was determined to show my all-around game." Everyone seemed to take notice. He became just the second player ever to lead the league in scoring and make the NBA all-defensive team. Eventually he became the first ever to lead the league in scoring and be named the NBA Defensive Player of the Year. Bulls' assistant coach John Bach put such an accomplishment in proper perspective by simply saying, "He is truly remarkable."

In the picture of Michael Jordan taking off from the foul line and gliding in for his winning jam in the 1988 NBA Slam Dunk Contest, Isiah Thomas is standing in the lower left corner with his fist clenched and his mouth hanging wide open. The NBA All-Star weekend in Chicago provided Jordan a chance to leave all his peers with a similar feeling. Isiah realized that if you can't beat him, join him, so the Detroit passing whiz set up the show for Jordan to be the star. He did nothing but turn heads by scoring 40 points on 17-of-23 shot-making, many of the lean-in, off-balance, off-the-glass variety.

In the first game after the All-Star break, Jordan was held to 20 points in an 89–74 loss at Detroit. Don't worry, be happy. Michael wasn't merely human; he was only tired. The rest of the season, Jordan put up numbers that continue to evoke awe to this day.

The scoreboard couldn't even keep up with Jordan. He had 46 at Cleveland, 36 at Philly, 38 at the Garden in New York and another 38 against the Cavaliers at home. On April 6, the headline in the *Chicago Tribune* beamed "Jordan Held to 29 points in loss to Washington." Still, magnificent Michael averaged 38 points over the last 14 games, six of which were wins on the road. The last victory of the season came at home over Boston and was the Bulls' 50th of the season.

Nevertheless, Jordan was still saving his best for last. The late-season surge earned the Bulls the third seed in the Eastern Conference of the 1988 NBA playoff tournament. They drew Cleveland in the best-of-five opening-round series. The Cavaliers were no match for Jordan—literally. In the second quarter of Game One in Chicago Stadium, Michael ran off for 20 points. Cleveland had 19. Michael finished the 104–93 victory with 50 points, and Collins said, "This was his finest defensive game since I've been here."

In that game, Jordan tied or set six team playoff records. After scoring 55 points to lead the Bulls to a 106–101 victory in Game Two, Jordan had two NBA records and 14 team records for the playoffs. Among his records were points in a regulation game (55), field goal attempts in a game (45), field goal attempts in a half (25), field goals made in a game (24), field goals made in a half (14) and steals in a quarter (3). "There is no quote you can give that would be good enough to describe what he has done," said Bulls' guard John Paxson. "It would only ruin it by my trying to tell you how I feel about it." Added teammate Scottie Pippen: "Michael Jordan is God's gift to the world." And finally Bach said: "We went to our Archangel offense. That's where we give the ball to Jordan and say 'Save us, Michael.'"

Cleveland held Jordan to 38 and 44 points when the series went back to Richfield for Games Three and Four. Jordan came on with 39 in the fifth and final game, a 107–101 Chicago victory that gave the Bulls the series. His 226 points were the most for a five-game playoff and it translated into a 45.2 per-game average. Such numbers were nowhere to be found as the Bulls lost in the next round of the playoffs to the Pistons in five games. In fact, the only significant digit from this series was three, as in the three defenders Detroit used on Michael whenever he touched the ball.

But that may have been the number which mattered most to Jordan. It took three players to shut him down. Two weren't enough. Was there a player more valuable than Michael in the NBA this season? Finally on May 25, 1988 Michael Jordan was named the NBA's Most Valuable Player. He received 47 first-place votes, which was 31 more than runner-up Larry Bird. Michael averaged 35 points, six assists and five rebounds, but it wasn't the numbers which made him the MVP. Detroit Pistons' coach Chuck Daly collected his chin off the Silverdome floor and explained why Michael was the best. "He's superhuman. I don't know how he does it, where he gets the energy. I'm telling you, the people of Chicago: You're seeing something there that only comes around once in a lifetime."

Tell us something we don't know, Chuck. Just when we thought we had seen it all, Jordan would show us something new. The Bulls won six straight games in the 1988 exhibition season as Michael picked up where he left off the previous year. But aside from his decision to skip the NBA slam-dunk contest at All-Star weekend, the only new news about Jordan in the 1988–89 season came when he failed to score 35 points or do something superheroic to pull out another victory. What could Michael do now that was really eye-opening?

How about not playing? Jordan was cruising along so smoothly during the 1988–89 season that his play urged Paxson to comment, "It must be like the rest of us playing with grade-school kids. That's how good he is." On March 7, 1989 Jordan suffered a groin injury that forced him out of the next game against the Celtics. It was the first game Michael had missed since the season-on-the-brink in 1985–86 when he sat out 64 games with a broken foot. But the pain in Jordan's groin proved to be a thorn in the side of the rest of the NBA.

Upon his return one game after the Bulls lost to the Celtics, Jordan cut down on his air raids on the rim and turned into a passing fancy. He scored but 18 points against Seattle Mar. 11, but he passed off for 15 assists. This proved to be a changing of the guards for the Bulls. In the next game, Jordan went from the shooting guard to the point guard and struck for 21 points, 14 assists and 14 rebounds in a 122–90 rout of Indiana. Said Jordan: "The way I've been playing the last two games is the way I'll play the rest of the season."

Michael was about to make a point to everyone who had thought they had seen everything. As the point guard, Jordan would have the ball instead of having to free himself from two or three defenders to get it. If the defense came right at him, he would deftly dish to Scottie Pippen or Craig Hodges for a perimeter jumper. In his first three games at the point—all victories—Michael averaged 22.3 points, 13.3 assists and 9.3 rebounds. Magical numbers, you might say; indeed Michael was now soaring like a Bird. Said Jordan: "I'm the kind of person who will do whatever he needs to for the team to win."

Winning, you see, was everything to Michael. So he recorded a career-high 17 assists to go with 33 points in a 128–113 win at Portland that made the Bulls 6–2 since Jordan took the point. That was the start of a West Coast swing in which the Bulls went 4–0 and Jordan struck for three triple-doubles. Jordan's sixth triple-double in seven games made the club 8–2 since the switch. In his first 17 games at the point, Jordan posted nine triple-doubles and helped the Bulls up their record to 45–30.

In its April 17 issue, *Sports Illustrated* pointed out that Jordan had paced the team to two wins over the Lakers and that the Pistons' holding him to an average of 27.6 points, 8.5 rebounds and 9 assists in six games constituted stopping Michael. The magazine continued to point out that the move to the point had alleviated the one argument against him: that he failed to make his teammates better. The fact of the matter remained that the Bulls were in the thick of the playoff battle without a bunch of guys named Kareem or Worthy or McHale or Parish. Then, *SI* argued that Jordan would not win the league's MVP award at the end of the season.

He did not; Magic Johnson did in the closest voting for the award in 10 years. *The Sporting News* gave the award to Jordan again for the calendar year 1988-89. Jordan didn't care one way or the other. "I'm more interested in winning a championship," he said.

Perhaps to prove the media wrong or to prove how great he could be, or perhaps just to leave everyone with one final reason to be caught mouth hanging open wide, Jordan put the Bulls on his back in the 1989 playoffs and carried them to winning they had never known the likes of before.

The regular season ended with a 90-84 loss to Cleveland, the same Cavaliers who as the third-seed would meet the sixth-seeded Bulls in the opening round of the Eastern Conference playoffs of the NBA post-season tournament. What a difference a year makes. Well, not exactly. Anyone who knew anything predicted the Bulls would lose the best-of-five series by getting swept in three straight games. Jordan came soaring in for a cradle jam off the break to give the Bulls a 20-point lead at the end of the third quarter, ran back upcourt by the press table and promptly shouted, "Sweep my butt." After losing Game Two, the Bulls came back to take Game Three 101-94 on 44 points from Jordan.

The next night he appeared on "Late Night with David Letterman," which was in town for the week, and announced that the series would not return to Cleveland for a fifth and final game. With nine seconds left, Michael stepped up to the foul line having already scored 50 points. The Bulls led 99–97. His would-be 51st point rimmed in and out. Cleveland won 108–105 in overtime after Jordan fouled out. After the game Jordan sat with James Jordan and said, "Daddy, I promise you I will never miss in that situation again." Perhaps then, the fifth game was set up for vindication, if not for network television. With six seconds left, Jordan hit a fall-away jumper over Larry Nance to give the Bulls a 99–98 lead. The Cavaliers' Craig Ehlo scored to make it 100–99, but Ehlo's last movement of the game would be a vain attempt to block Jordan's last shot. Instead, he just sat there with his mouth hanging open as the shot fell through. Forget eyebrows; this was a hair-raising experience.

"I never saw the shot go in," Michael said, "but I knew right away from the crowd reaction—silence —that it was good." Sometimes reactions speak louder than words.

There really are no more words left to describe what Jordan went on to accomplish in his fifth pro season. He averaged 37 points as the Bulls beat the New York Knicks in six games in the Eastern Conference semifinals. He scored 40 points, had 15 rebounds and nine assists, and reinjured his groin in a Game Three win in Chicago. Then he scored 42, including two free throws with six seconds left as the Bulls closed out the series in

Game Six. Michael had 33 points and 11 rebounds as the Bulls stole Game One of the Eastern Finals in Detroit, 94–88. But he still had one last shot to take.

The series came to Chicago for the third game, and the Bulls were trailing by 14 points with 6:30 to go in the fourth quarter. Jordan proceeded to score 17 of his 46 points in the next 6:26. With nine seconds left, he took an inbound pass from Pippen, drove to his right and drove the Pistons' Dennis Rodman back on his heels, then pulled up about eight feet from the basket. Isiah came over to help, but Jordan banked in a hook for a 99–97 victory.

"It was a very special shot," Michael said. It would be the easiest shot he would come by the rest of the series, save for a double clutch two-hand jam over Rodman in Game Four that will surely be the lead highlight on "NBA Action is Fan-Tastic" commercials for the next couple of seasons. Eventually, the Pistons formulated a special defense called "Jordan rules" to stop this one-man bandit. The strategy featured little more than Joe Dumars leading a bevy of defenders at Michael at all times. He scored 73 points in the next three games, and took just eight shots in Game Four of the series. For this season, for this point in his career that was stopping Jordan.

But he still led the Bulls to within two victories of the 1989 NBA Finals, and judging by the way the Pistons manhandled the Lakers, perhaps that far away from a world championship. In the process, he managed to attract the attention of the entire nation. Imagine America's basketball fans sitting in their living rooms with mouths dropped slightly open and eyebrows raised to the limit. There goes Michael, spinning and grinning and scooping the ball between his legs and off his tongue into the hoop.

Unfathomable, simply unfathomable.

16.

There Goes Mr. Jordan

HERE ARE SOME FINAL WORDS ABOUT MI-
chael Jeffrey Jordan.

For all of his super-heroic tendencies, Jordan
perhaps longs to be merely human. He wishes he
were like you and me, so he can go see *Indiana
Jones and the Last Crusade* without having to call
the theater, arrive 10 minutes after the start and
leave 10 minutes before the end in order to avoid
making a scene. But, then, privacy is a precious
commodity for a man who paid more than $10,000
in fines during the 1987–88 season because he
attracts so much of a crowd at the airport he cannot
make the team's preflight deadline of being at the
gate 30 minutes before takeoff. He goes to a major
league baseball game, and those who spend most of
their time signing autographs turn and ask Michael
for his.

So Jordan forsakes his private life for refuge on
the golf course. He spends 8 to 10 hours a day
there during the offseason, because "When I'm on

the golf course, I'm at peace." What privacy Michael does take for himself, he secures by wearing dark glasses and moving very quickly in public.

Otherwise, Jordan can easily be found lying on the couch in the Chapel Hill, N.C., apartment belonging to Adolph Shiver, Michael's main man. Adolph is one of the home boys, the guys Michael runs with and hangs with and calls when he's on the road and lonely or just passing time. Shiver is in real estate, and the rest of this gang includes Fred Kearns, a mortician, and Fred Whitfield, a lawyer.

Michael says he loves these guys, and they love him. They know just how far to push Michael. They can razz and tease and beat him at Blackjack or take his money playing pool. But they know when he says take off your shoes before walking on my brand new living room carpet that Michael isn't talking trash. They come and stay with Michael at his luxurious home in Highland Park, a suburb of Chicago, because "Without these guys I could easily go crazy." Michael says, "I try to be with them at all times. They make me feel more at home, more human, more down to earth."

About that house, by the way. Highland Park is a very well-to-do, predominantly Jewish town which may have Michael because of its four golf courses. People in town are very fond of having Michael as a neighbor, and one of the most treasured secrets is knowing which house he actually lives in. About that house: well, for one thing the white Porsche 911 Turbo, the Midnight Blue Mercedes with the UNC 23 license plate or the black Corvette with JUMP 23—or all three—are often parked in front.

The featured attraction in the house undoubtedly is the basement which *Sports Illustrated*'s Jack

McCallum described in a March 13, 1989 article as an "adult day-care center." Deluxe stereo system, large-screen TV, pool table, ping-pong table, poker table and six-hole artificial putting green make up what might be better described as an adult amusement park. And perhaps this is the key to Michael Jordan—that he has a lot of little kid in him, and in that respect he is just like you and me. This is the side of Jordan that he is always striving to maintain, yet likes to keep away from the bright lights.

Jordan's best side is the one "60 Minutes" and movie producers and even "Miami Vice" are after. Imagine Michael taking Crockett and Tubbs to the hoop? When Hollywood was casting the movie version of Rick Telander's book *Heaven is a Playground*, producers came up with an offer of $50,000 for a cameo role. Pro-Serv wanted a six-figure deal. They said they could get Isiah for 50 grand. Pro-Serv said go get him. Eventually Jordan signed on for $400,000.

When Diane Sawyer and "60 Minutes" trailed Michael around for a segment in January of 1987, it made for one of the show's most successful pieces. Sawyer has since confessed her infatuation with Michael, but whether it be live or in person, Jordan cannot deny the powerful effect he has on women. Here was a guy who took home economics classes in high school to prepare for life as a bachelor, then at the 1984 Summer Olympics he and U.S. swimmer Kim Gallagher became such a hot item that Bobby Knight almost discovered her while checking his players' rooms at curfew. (Gallagher hid in the closet just before Knight came in.)

So Michael became a renowned ladies' man.

There was the tale of Robin Givens, who threatened to turn Jordan into Mike Tyson. "It got tired in five or six days," Michael said. "I could see it." Well, that may have been one woman who wanted Michael for his money. The woman Jordan trusts most is his mother, who still comes to town and cooks Michael's pre-game steak-and-eggs. He was supposed to be married, but he broke off that year-long engagement. His family includes his parents, his main men and his son Jeffrey Michael, who was born in December, 1988.

Despite the stardom, Jordan is determined to remain unaffected. His appreciation for the little things in life adds to his tremendous luster. For Halloween, 1986, Jordan asked McDonald's to print up cards with his name on them for free Big Macs to give to trick-or-treaters. Alas, the Bulls were out of town that night, but if you happen to be in the neighborhood this Halloween, kids, drop by Michael's place. You'll never have a Big Mac attack like this!

Now, more than ever, seems to be the right time for Michael to deliver a message to those fans he considers his most ardent supporters. If there are all those kids out there who want to grow up to be like Michael Jordan, you don't need drugs to sky. During his rookie season, Michael was just trying to be friendly when he burst in on some teammates who were in the midst of partying. "Enjoy," he said, then turned around and walked out. As he sits atop the basketball world, Michael's biggest worry is falling off because of such a mishap. This, however, may be something for Michael to put into his own words.

"You know, I scored 13 points in a game against

Washington, and it was my worst game in the NBA. That could have been the perfect time to go out and get drunk or get involved with something I'm not supposed to. Instead, I had dinner with my attorney. I blocked it out of my mind. I know I'm only human, and I've got that inner confidence to put that behind me. The things that scare me most are the bad things that would tear down Michael Jordan's image. But my lifestyle is so positive that I'm not afraid of something from my past coming back to haunt me. I live a clean, healthy life, and I'm happy about it. I've never done drugs, and I've never had a reason to do drugs."

Jordan's only addiction in life is to the game of golf. In fact, much of life after basketball will no doubt be lived on a golf course or two. Davis Love, the PGA touring pro from North Carolina, hooked Jordan on the game when both were in college. Michael stepped up to the tee for the first time and promptly whiffed at the ball. But then he managed a couple of good shots. "And you know how golf is. That's all you need to keep coming back. I've been coming back ever since."

Jordan's golfing is becoming legendary. During the 1988 basketball season, he was posing for a poster at a Chicago health club for Nike, and in between photo shoots he could be found at the indoor driving range. His shots off the tee are often as breathtaking as his shots on the court. He can drive the ball up to 300 yards. "If only I could hit it straight," he said. "Maybe I could get real good at it. Practice hard, and play for five years until I'm thirty-seven, then join the PGA Seniors tour at fifty."

Practice by day and night was all that Michael

did during the summer of 1987, '88 and '89. All the time he used to spend hooping during the summer now goes into golf. In 1988, he cut his handicap to an 8, and posted a personal best round of 74. The rating on Jordan according to one golf pro: good putter, good middle irons and erratic off the tee.

Michael Jordan will forever work on his game of golf, his game of basketball and his game of life until he is all he can be. He already is the best-dressed player in the NBA, having been voted so by the rest of the players during the 1989 All-Star weekend in Houston. Doesn't it seem like the more we know about Michael, the more we have to shake our heads and say, "no way, man"? How can anyone seem so incredible?

But he's real, totally real. When all is said and done, Michael Jordan is the greatest.

17.

Appendix:
Glossary of Jordan-ology

Alley-oop: A lob, perfectly timed pass from a player on the perimeter to a player leaping toward the basket. The ball is thrown over the defending players and often results in a basket, sometimes a slam dunk.

Back-door: The side of the basket away from the ball. If the back door is open, opportunity knocks for a sure hoop, sometimes even an alley-oop slam dunk.

Baseline: Technically speaking, the baselines mark off either end of the basketball court. Has been redefined recently, though, to mean in the direction toward the basket, as in "I'm going baseline."

Drop-step: A quick step used to fake a defender one way, then turn and go the other way on him.

Fallaway or fadeaway J: A jump shot taken while your momentum and your body are moving away from the basket and you're on your way to falling down.

Game: When it is used at "the game," the reference is to the game of basketball as in "Jordan is the best in the game." Other references are to a player's ability, as "I'm really on top of my game."

Guru: One who knows so much about the game that his opinions are the authority on the subject of the conversation.

Hang time: The amount of elapsed time a given object or person continuously soars at the peak of flight. Has been shortened to hang, as in "Hey, bro, did you see me hang on that fadeaway J?"

Home boys: Your best friends from your hometown who knew you way back when and will always be your friends.

Hoop: A basket or the basket, as in the "rack."

In your face: A move or a shot so superb it nets one the karma of face. Usually a payback on the court. After someone points his finger at you or starts talking trash, you come down the court, pop a 20-foot jumper over the man in question and say to him, "In your face."

Jam: A dunk.

Jam master: The guy on the court who can dunk better than anybody else.

Megastar: Someone whose personal magnitude is so great that he or she can't be grouped with the other, ordinary stars. The realm of Magic, Bird, Kareem, and perhaps Joan Collins.

Paytonesque: Used to describe something so superlative no other words suffice, derived from Walter Payton, the Chicago Bears running back who is the greatest to ever play the game of football. Something Paytonesque is so good it is better than the best.

Player: Perhaps the highest compliment that can be paid to someone who is on top of his game. Used by itself, to say someone is a player means he can do it all—shoot, pass, and dribble the rock.

Rack: The basket. The game is played under the rack.

Rock: A name for the basketball, used primarily in the midst of the game to communicate with a teammate, as in "Hey man, throw me the rock, I've got a shot."

Synergy: What happens when you add one and one and one and get five.

Talking trash: Words of provocation on the court that make a player pick up his game and come back down to pop a jumper in the face of the guy who was talking trash.

Triple-double: When a player records double figures in any three statistical categories in a single game—usually points, rebounds, and assists.

THE SILENCE OF THE LAMBS

THE ELECTRIFYING BESTSELLER BY

THOMAS HARRIS

" THRILLERS DON'T COME ANY BETTER THAN THIS."
—CLIVE BARKER

"HARRIS IS QUITE SIMPLY THE BEST SUSPENSE NOVELIST
WORKING TODAY." — *The Washington Post*

Exciting Lives—
Memorable People
from St. Martin's Press!